Advance Praise for
Beyond the Green Widow

"An engaging story about the journey Juanita takes to uncover the mysterious shroud surrounding the murder of her grandfather, Jake Green. Through tireless research and perseverance, she pieces together the full puzzle of her family history. This book provides valuable insight into the history of the prohibition era in Greene County."

—ARRIXIE GARRETSON SPROUL
INTERIM DIRECTOR OF GREENE COUNTY MUSEUM

"I was so impressed with the book. The research and detail was amazing. If not for your and Juanita's efforts, I would have completed my thirty-two-year career in alcohol law enforcement and not know about the murder of these two fine men. This book definitely gets two thumbs up!!! Well done, ladies!!!!"

—JOEY MILES, AGENT-IN-CHARGE
MISSISSIPPI ALCOHOLIC BEVERAGE CONTROL

"*Beyond the Green Widow: Consequences of the Piney Woods Creek Murders of 1921* is a fantastic read and a wonderful tribute to heroes gunned down in their prime by Mississippi moonshiners. Juanita Green Hollinghead weaves a fantastic story detailing her research and dogged determination to discover the facts about her grandfather, Jacob Green's, murder. Green was a Special Agent of the Internal Revenue Service "Prohibition Unit." Today, this "unit" is known as the Bureau of Alcohol, Tobacco, Firearms and Explosives. Green, along with Richton Mississippi Town Marshal Lawrence Dunnam, was murdered during a raid on an illegal liquor still deep in the southern Mississippi woods.

As a retired ATF Special Agent myself, I applaud the writer for her commitment, perseverance and determination to recognize the heroic efforts of her ancestor and Marshal Dunnam. Too often, those who have come before us and made the ultimate sacrifice are overlooked. Forgotten by today's hustle and bustle and the ever-changing headlines. Today's ATF Special Agents are no longer raiding stills and chasing moonshiners. The product has changed. Today, ATF Special Agents are pursuing gun smugglers, bomb makers, drug dealers, and the most violent criminals on the street. The Bureau of Alcohol, Tobacco, Firearms and Explosives has a rich history of enforcing unpopular laws, often, as Juanita Green Hollinghead discovers, to the detriment of its agents and their families.

Thank you, Juanita Green Hollinghead, for taking the time to pen this tribute to the heroes that came before."

—JAMES LANGLEY
ATF ASSOCIATION OF RETIREES EXECUTIVE DIRECTOR

"Law enforcement, whether federal, state, or local, is inherently dangerous for the professionals who perform their responsibilities. Juanita Hollinghead personally understands this as she poignantly tells the story of her grandfather's career and ultimate sacrifice in the line of duty and honor. We professionals willingly choose this career to protect our families, communities, and country.

Beyond the Green Widow: Consequences of the Piney Woods Creek Murders of 1921 provides a heartfelt true story of sacrifice and the danger facing all law enforcement and the effect on their families. Juanita Hollinghead's and Sherye Green's presentation is impactful in its detail of the costs of duty. It underscores how the impact of a law enforcement professional's death in the line of duty reverberates for generations on the families and communities who endure it.

This book is a must-read story that honors and cements this sacrifice. *We must never forget!"*

—SHAN L. KIRK
SENIOR SPECIAL AGENT – RETIRED
UNITED STATES SECRET SERVICE

"When a law officer dies in the line of duty, it affects not only his or her family but the community as a whole. We simply don't expect good people sworn to protect us to be overcome by the evils of our world. It makes us fearful of what evil lies in waiting for us. Stories such as the one of Jake Green help us to remember. Remember what good men will do in the face of evil. Remember what happens when evil wins for a moment. Tragedy often produces legacy, and from the stories of men like Agent Jake Green, we can learn to win battles against evil in our communities. Rules, procedures, and technology have certainly changed how our communities are policed since 1921. Still, when an officer loses the battle and doesn't come home to his family, the consequences are unfortunately the same. We must preserve the memories of our past heroes to allow the families left behind to mourn and begin the healing process after their passing. We must also celebrate their life of sacrificial service to guarantee our safety and security."

—CHIEF (RET.) LUKE THOMPSON, POLICE CHIEF FOR
CITY OF BYRAM, MISSISSIPPI

"Juanita Hollinghead's desire to know the factual details surrounding her grand-father's death led her to do an exhaustive search into the activities of that fateful day. Her excellent writing skills and integrity in portraying the true story make this book an excellent choice for the reader. Sherye Green handles her subject matter and characters like in her day-to-day relationships—with honesty, care, and grace. It is no wonder she has been sought out to tell the stories of people who have lived in the best and worst circumstances. I gladly recommend *Beyond the Green Widow*."

—JAMES ARRINGTON GOFF
THE NEWS-COMMERCIAL
OUR SOUTH MAGAZINE

"As the CEO of the National Law Enforcement Officers Memorial Fund, I have the privilege of walking the sacred walls of the Law Enforcement Memorial in Washington, D.C., almost daily. Every single time I do, I'm humbled to be surrounded by the 23,785 (*and counting) names of the nation's law enforcement heroes who have died in the line of duty. Amongst those names, nestled on panel 16 West, line 12, is the name of Jacob Francis Green. Special Agent Jake Green was one of the very first agents for what went on to become the Bureau of Alcohol, Tobacco, Firearms and Explosives (ATF). He was also one of the first such agents to die in the line of duty, as he was shot and killed in 1921 during a raid on an illegal whiskey still. I've long believed that the men and women called to the profession of law enforcement represent something much more than a single thread woven into the fabric of the communities they commit their lives to. The story of Jake, his tragic death, and the staggering and enduring impact of his loss on both his family and his community serves to perfectly illustrate the profound impact every single law enforcement death represents.

Researched and written by Jake's granddaughter, Juanita Green Hollinghead, *Beyond the Green Widow: Consequences of the Piney Woods Creek Murders of 1921*, is a masterful narrative that not only recounts a pivotal moment in Mississippi's history during the tumultuous era of Prohibition but also offers a deeply personal exploration of the horrible aftermath the tragedy had on generations of the Green family.

Juanita and co-author Sherye Green have meticulously woven together family history, local lore, and extensive research to walk the reader through the events before and after Jake's death. Through that narrative, they allow us into the heart of a family forever altered by the loss of their patriarch, particularly the widow Eliza Green, who was forced to navigate the world as both a widow and a single mother in an era that offered little support for women in her position.

Beyond the Green Widow is a compelling reminder of the sacrifices made by law enforcement officers and their families. Jake's story demonstrates the long shadow cast by loss and the power of storytelling to preserve our shared history. There is a quote by President George Bush on the southwest corner of the Memorial, which begins with 'Carved on these walls is the Story of America.' Juanita Green Hollinghead and Sherye S. Green have told one small part of the continuing American story here, serving as both a poignant family memoir and a valuable contribution to the history of U.S. law enforcement."

—WILLIAM ALEXANDER
CHIEF EXECUTIVE OFFICER
NATIONAL LAW ENFORCEMENT OFFICERS MEMORIAL FUND

"In 1972, when I applied to be an ATF Special Agent, one of the people who interviewed me said that ATF had more of its agents killed than any other federal agency. He explained that most of these deaths occurred during the time that the predecessors of today's ATF investigated moonshine stills. Though I never had the opportunity to work on this type of case, Juanita Hollinghead's well-researched and well-written book, *Beyond the Green Widow*, allowed a fascinating glimpse into that world. In addition to writing about the murder of her grandfather, Hollinghead provides a unique and complete overview of the investigation and prosecution of the men who killed her grandfather. An added benefit is the insight into how this crime affected her family and how she discovered and developed a wealth of pertinent information, some over a century old."

—JO ANN C. KOCHER, ATF ASSISTANT
SPECIAL AGENT IN CHARGE (RETIRED)
FIRST FEMALE ATF SPECIAL AGENT
FORMER PRESIDENT, ATF ASSOCIATION

Beyond the Green Widow

Consequences of the
Piney Woods Creek Murders of 1921

Juanita Green Hollinghead
with Sherye S. Green

SUNBURY
P R E S S ®

Mechanicsburg, PA USA

Published by Sunbury Press, Inc.
Mechanicsburg, Pennsylvania

SUNBURY
P R E S S
www.sunburypress.com

For information about special discounts for bulk purchases, please contact Sunbury Press Orders Dept. at (855) 338-8359 or orders@sunburypress.com.

To request one of our authors for speaking engagements or book signings, please contact Sunbury Press Publicity Dept. at publicity@sunburypress.com.

FIRST SUNBURY PRESS EDITION: November 2024

Set in Adobe Garamond | Interior design by Crystal Devine | Cover by Lawrence Knorr | Edited by Amanda Krieger and Anaya Montgomery.

Publisher's Cataloging-in-Publication Data
Names: Hollinghead, Juanita Green, author | Green, Sherye S., author.
Title: Beyond the green widow : consequences of the Piney Woods Creek murders of 1921 / Juanita Green Hollinghead with Sherye S. Green.
Description: First trade paperback edition. | Mechanicsburg, PA : Sunbury Press, 2024.
Summary: The 1921 April Fool's Day murders of U.S. Treasury Special Agent Jacob "Jake" Green and Richton Town Marshal Lawrence Dunnam rocked the citizens of two sleepy little Mississippi towns to their cores. As the officers arrived to arrest several local men operating an illegal liquor still, four men lay in wait for them. Someone had tipped off the moonshiners. Author Juanita Green Hollinghead, a granddaughter Jake never lived to know, brings to life this riveting account of the true-crime event that shaped her family's history.
Identifiers: ISBN 979-8-88819-252-8 (softcover).
Subjects: BIOGRAPHY & AUTOBIOGRAPHY / Law Enforcement | HISTORY / United States & Local / South (AL, AR, FL, GA, KY, LA, MS, NC, SC, TN, VA, WV) | TRUE CRIME / Historical.

Designed in the USA
0 1 1 2 3 5 8 13 21 34 55

For the Love of Books!

These pages are dedicated to a man I never knew,
who lived decades before me,
in a time where the consequences of his choices
have trickled down to me, his youngest grandchild.
I have been inspired to share the story of his life and death,
before it was lost in an old leather satchel and a brown paper sack.

Nobody knew what those bags held . . . until now.

Why?

Pausing in the present, to allow one to
hold on to the past,
to enable one to
preserve for the future,
so the
journey will never be forgotten.

That's why . . .

—Juanita Green Hollinghead

TABLE OF CONTENTS

Foreword

I CANNOT fathom a world without the preservation of history. A place to visit to see who we were, who we are, and who we are likely to be. History allows us to stand on the same ground yet travel to a previously existing time. The storytellers of history are invaluable to our culture, our identity, and to our communities. Juanita Green Hollinghead is a storyteller. She preserves for our generation and generations to come a story of perseverance, love, and sacrifice. In *Beyond the Green Widow: Consequences of the Piney Woods Creek Murders of 1921*, Hollinghead preserves a valuable part of our history for all of us.

As an almost lifelong Greene Countian (I moved to the southern tip of Heaven when I was five years old), I have known the Green family for most of my life. The Green family leads by example. This family exemplifies love, generosity, and commitment to each other and the place we call home. *Beyond the Green Widow* is an important story. This story needed to be told, and it also needs to be read by not only Greene Countians and Mississippians but by all who value history and believe in hope and determination.

When Jacob "Jake" Francis Green was shot and killed while raiding a whiskey still on April 1, 1921, history was watching. The time of Prohibition (a constitutional ban on the manufacture, transportation, and sale of alcohol) in America was unique and volatile. Law enforcement officers were presented with a dangerous task. Although the supply of alcohol was curtailed, the demand remained. Thus, whisky stills, which were not unique, became a tool to supply that demand. And officers like Jake Green were sworn to uphold the law and enforce Prohibition. And in doing so, Jake Green lost his life, and the lives of all in the Green family were impacted forever.

Eliza Green became a widow on April 1, 1921, and stood in the wide gap left by the death of her beloved husband. She devoted herself to her children and family. The selflessness and commitment demonstrated by Jake and Eliza Green live today through their many descendants. One of those descendants is Juanita Green Hollinghead, the writer of this story. Through many years of life experience and research, Hollinghead presents a story that will educate and encourage—a tale that history made and needed preserving.

I am happy she wrote this history . . . and you will be, too.

Randy Pierce
Former Mississippi Supreme Court Justice
Leakesville, Mississippi

Introduction

MY earliest recollection of my paternal grandfather, Jacob "Jake" Francis Green, whom I respectfully refer to as Granddaddy Green, was Momma sharing with us kids the importance of us not asking Daddy about his father's death. She told us that Jake had gotten shot and killed while he and another officer were raiding a whiskey still when my dad was only six years old. My grandfather's sudden absence was tough on the family he left behind. Sadly, my great-grandfather, Franklin James Green, had died of pneumonia only a few months before his son's tragic death.

1921 was a devastating year for our family. Coming to terms with the loss of two pillars of this strong family dying within months of each other was almost too much for the living to comprehend. Family and friends had to continue living in a world without two of the men they so loved and respected. Eliza, my Grandmother Green, also called "Mimi" by her grandchildren, never married again. After Jake's death, it was as if a stone rolled over Mimi's heart, and from that time on, this broken-hearted woman shared no more love in the Jake Green home. She pulled her children closer into her tangled web as she began this new season as a widow. For as long as I can remember, "Widow" is what my father called his mother.

Because Jake, my Granddaddy Green, had been murdered on April Fool's Day, my siblings and I were not allowed to tell April Fool's jokes in our household. We were also never allowed to ask questions about our grandfather's death. However, it was something about which we wondered a great deal. As the anniversary of Jake's death would pass year after year, this silent remembrance stifled us all. By the time I reached elementary age, I had told my classmates I could not play jokes on April Fool's Day because moonshiners had killed my granddaddy on that day. While not participating in any April Fool's Day antics kept me out of trouble, I carried on the Green tradition of silence about that day. My dad and I shared a special bond that I treasure; even so, I never mentioned the subject of his father to him. I honored that request until he died.

April Fool's Day, 1921. A day in Mississippi's history when my father's mother, Eliza, became a widow and when my father and his two siblings became fatherless statistics in a simple world of faith, family, and moral integrity. A man I never knew fell to his death, fulfilling his sworn obligation to uphold justice and keep the dreadful moonshine manufacturing as limited as possible. Mimi began her journey as the Widow Green on that not-so-foolish Friday morning—never marrying again and rearing three young children, ages nine, six, and five, with little or no assistance. Boldly bitter, Mimi would survive and live the remainder of her life as the "Green Widow."

I was born forty-two years after my grandfather's death. As Jake and Eliza's youngest grandchild, I have felt a heart-wrenching burden to investigate and research further the accounts of events leading up to and after Jake's murder. Because I was never allowed to speak about this nightmarish event during my childhood, I wanted all of Jake's offspring to know his role in Mississippi's history. He was one of the inaugural officers appointed Revenuer when Prohibition began in 1920.

The watershed event of my grandfather's death on April Fool's Day, 1921, has guided me to this day. With pen in hand, I want to take you back to a previous century and reveal this agonizing story's elements—when, what, where, why, and how. As Eliza wove a tangled web of anguish after losing her Forever Jacob, she became the webmaster of her little world. My grandmother remained the Green Widow until her death on July 30, 1987, at ninety-six years of age. Mimi lived her life far *Beyond the Green Widow!*

This story began on April 1st, 1921, on the Piney Woods Creek on the Greene-Perry County line in south Mississippi: the raiding of a whiskey still, bullets flying, men dying, and families crying. Growing up, I often pondered the details surrounding my grandfather's death. All I knew was what Momma had shared and from reading his obituary from the *Greene County Herald*, plus a few other newspaper clippings. Every time I drove across Piney Woods Creek on Highway 42, I would wonder exactly where the murder occurred.

The Greene County Courthouse was the hub of everyday life in our community of Leakesville, Mississippi. Since the mid-1800s, several courthouse buildings have been burned or torn down. Once the county constructed the existing courthouse building in 1939, the original jailhouse remained behind the new structure for many years. Finally, when the old jail was condemned and torn down, Momma retrieved a few bricks from the ruins. I ended up with one of them.

Courthouse connections run deep with me.

Before I was born, my dad was the Sheriff of Greene County. His office was in the courthouse. Mr. Williams was sheriff in that courthouse. My mother's extension office job worked out of the courthouse. This historic building was where some of the most important research for this book was conducted.

Like his father, my daddy also served as the sheriff of Greene County. Daddy shared that when he was in office in 1947, he planted the magnolia trees around the courthouse that still stand today. At the time, he had to construct a small fence around each tree to keep free-range cattle from destroying them as they grew.

The courthouse also had many special memories for me that became part of my life's story. When I was five years old, I befriended Mr. Sydney Williams. At the time, he was the local butcher at Turner's Grocery in Leakesville, and my mother and I would see him when she went shopping. While shopping one day with my mother, I asked Mr. Sydney for a job. He promised me one if I would get my social security number, which a six-year-old was not required to do in 1969.

My card finally arrived in the mail one day in 1970, the year I was in first grade, and I could not wait to share the news with Mr. Sydney. He had received a promotion during the period I was waiting for my card. He had run for and was elected Greene County's newest sheriff. Momma said I could go after school and show the card to him, possibly to cash in on his promise of a job. At that time, it was safe for a six-year-old to walk from our house to the courthouse, and I did so every chance I could. The sheriff's office was on the Greene County Courthouse's main floor, near the building's south entrance—the first door on the left.

True to his word, Sheriff Williams assigned me a "job" working around the courthouse. I was one thrilled young child! When the sheriff would send me to take a note to the jailer on the fourth floor, I would always pause at the stairwell before entering this intimidating part of the Greene County Courthouse building. The jail was a separate building behind the old courthouse during my grandfather's lifetime.

Suspended above me, as high as my eyes could see, was a metal hook-like hanger from which would hang the rope for a prisoner's execution. Below it, on the floor, were two metal flaps that appeared to be able to pull apart to an opening below. This mechanism was the "hanging trap door" constructed in 1939 as part of the newer courthouse. The doors to the gallows would separate as a jailer pulled the lever and a convict's body would then drop into the opening during an execution. Capital punishment by hanging ended in Mississippi on October 11, 1940, when death by electrocution began.

Part of the story about one of the men that killed Granddaddy Green was that he was to have been hanged in the Greene County Jail. From an early age, I imagined this was where the execution might have taken place. I only knew bits and pieces of what happened in the dark forest along Piney Woods Creek. There were vague snatches of information about another of the convicted murderers who were to have committed suicide while incarcerated. I desperately wanted to know more but never asked Daddy, partly out of respect for him. The other part was out of fear of my father. He was very stern, as Mimi was. You did not question him. I also wanted to honor my momma, who had told me never to ask him about the murders because the subject was too sad to discuss.

At another time in my life, in 2005, the basement of the Greene County Courthouse flooded, where officials stored all older court documents. A small portion of the collection was salvaged and moved to higher ground to protect files from future water damage. Reverend James Dunnam, a distant cousin of Lawrence Dunnam, the other law enforcement officer killed alongside my grandfather, helped the Board of Supervisors renovate the old fourth-floor jail into the Greene County Museum and Historical Society in 2003. Surviving documents of the fires of earlier buildings or the flooded basement of this current one found a new home in the research rooms of the museum. Because I knew how much had been destroyed by the earlier fires and the flooding, I doubted I would have any luck searching for evidence regarding Granddaddy Green's death, so I never pursued investigating any remaining paperwork.

Over a century has passed since the death of my grandfather, Jake Green, and I'm paying tribute to this man. Shared within the pages of this book is the story of the choices he and all the others made on April Fool's Day of 1921. Since my father died in 1988, I have devoted myself to researching this true-crime event. The information discovered while on this journey has shed light on experiences and memories of my childhood.

Writing this book has been incredibly therapeutic, allowing me to let go of the deep obligation that has been a part of me for as long as I can remember. I have felt such closeness to my Granddaddy Green throughout the years, a feeling I can't quite explain. A heartfelt obligation drives me to share the legacy of his life that ended at thirty-seven years, four months, twenty-three days, and twelve hours.

God supplied me with His ever-present guidance throughout this journey. He orchestrated encounters allowing me to be in certain places at certain times, to meet specific individuals, and to uncover bits and pieces of this case that others would have otherwise forgotten. God showed up and showed out on my journey to discover the past, so I can share with the present and leave my grandfather's true legacy for the future.

So many tears . . .

Too soon . . .

Never to be forgotten . . .

My job is to ensure Granddaddy Green's legacy lives on forever by sharing his story.

Juanita Green Hollinghead
Leakesville, Mississippi
December 2024

PART I

Strands of the Web

"April Fool's Choices"

Law Men or Liquor Men
Both sides of a lawless coin
Heads you lost
Tails you lost
Foolish Choices!

—Juanita Green Hollinghead

CHAPTER ONE

The Jake Green Family Web

MY Green family roots go back five generations. My cousin, Dr. Byron E. Green, Jr., compiled a "Greene County History" family narrative many years ago. A careful study of this document has afforded me a greater understanding of my family's history and a deeper appreciation for the significant contributions many generations of Greens made while settling this portion of southeast Mississippi along the Chickasawhay River.

Greene County, where my hometown of Leakesville is located, was named for Revolutionary War hero Nathaniel Greene and was founded in 1811 while Mississippi was still a territory. Six years later, in 1817, Mississippi became America's twentieth state. Leakesville was incorporated in 1906 and named in honor of Walter Leake, Mississippi's third governor, who served from 1822 until 1825.

My great-great-grandfather, James Matthew "Woolsorter" Green, the first in our family to settle in this area, was born in Ireland in the late 1700s. Family history shares that by his early adult years, he was fluent in "nine languages" and had acquired training as a physician and a tinsmith. James, his brother Franklin, and two sisters came to the United States by ship. James paid for their passage while working aboard it as a butcher. The ship docked in the port of Charleston, South Carolina, and soon afterward, the siblings made their way to New York State. After the death of one of the sisters from a heart attack, the remaining siblings moved to Louisville, Kentucky.

In Kentucky, an unfortunate work accident took the life of my great-great grandfather's brother. At the time of his death, Franklin Green was a wealthy man, making money in construction. Franklin and his wife Amy, unable to have children, adopted a young boy. Sadly, once the boy became a man, his adoptive father, Franklin, died in an accident while building a new home for his family. Shortly afterward, the unnamed son murdered his adoptive mother, stole her money and precious possessions, set fire to the house, and disappeared. After his brother's death, James moved to Mobile, Alabama, where he became a successful merchant.

Calamity struck once more around 1850. A notorious band of robbers, the Copeland Gang, robbed James's store and set fire to the business. Forced to begin again, James then turned to his tin smithing skills by which to make his living, earning him the nickname "Tinner". Around this time, a yellow fever epidemic swept through the Mobile area.[1] Local Alabama history records state that Mobile citizens battled eleven outbreaks between 1819 and 1853. James decided to load his wagon with his tin wares and head in a northwesterly direction.

Upon finding a welcoming community in Mississippi, Tinner met and married Priscilla Moody, whose father was a local minister. The couple eventually settled in Washington, Mississippi, a small settlement later renamed Neely. (This small town is on the opposite side of the state from the first Washington, Mississippi, located in the southwestern corner of the state and which served as the second territorial capital before the state's admission to the Union.) Tinner and Priscilla had twelve children who lived to adulthood—seven sons and five daughters. Two other children were born but did not survive. My great-grandfather, Francis "Si" James Green, was one of those twelve.

Tinner served in the Civil War with four of Si's brothers; at age twelve, Si was too young to enlist. William, one of those four sons who went to war with Tinner, did not survive the conflict. After the Civil War, Tinner and his remaining sons returned home. Once reunited, Tinner and Priscilla worked hard to provide a good life for their family.

Si met and married Isadora "Iddie" Evelyn McClean on February 27, 1879. They settled into their new life together in Washington, as

Si was an established "merchant and farmer." The couple moved to Leakesville three years later, where he would later own and operate one of Leakesville's first general stores.

Iddie was the daughter of a steamship captain, Captain Jacob Fry McClean, and inherited her father's grit and courage. She also reflected the culture and softness of her mother, Mary Elizabeth Knight McClean. The latter had ensured her daughter received both language and music lessons—French and piano. The family's good standing afforded Iddie many invitations to parties and social events.

Stories say that my great-grandparents were an unforgettable couple, as Si was well over six feet tall, and Iddie did not even reach the five-foot mark. Iddie and Si had nine children—five sons and four daughters. My grandfather, Jacob "Jake" Francis Green, the third of these siblings and Si's and Iddie's first son, was born on January 3, 1884. My grandparents were also an unforgettable couple. My grandmother, Eliza Ellen Roberts, was born on July 24, 1891, in McLain, Mississippi, a small town seventeen miles west of Leakesville.

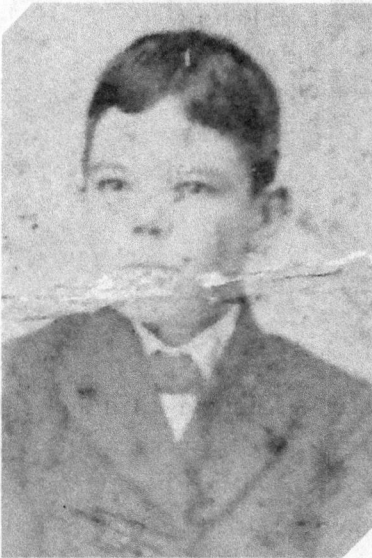

My grandfather, Jake, as a boy   My grandmother, Eliza, as a little girl

11

She and my grandfather met sometime in the late spring or early summer of 1910. A cousin of Eliza's arranged for her to meet Jake, as she thought they would make a sweet couple.

Dashing Jake Green

Eliza Roberts— the woman who captured Jake's heart

The young law enforcement official was quite a catch and cut a dashing figure—a trim, fit build at five feet, nine inches with brown wavy hair and dark brown eyes. Eliza, a dark-haired beauty, was considered a prize herself. Their first encounter was at a church revival in Neely. The plan the cousin devised to get them acquainted worked like a charm—it was love at first sight for these two, and they never looked back. Many said Jake stole the heart of one of Greene County's most charming young ladies.

Jake and Eliza with the Reverend Alex Breland on their wedding day

After courting Eliza Roberts for only a few months, Jake popped the question, and Eliza accepted. They got married in a private family ceremony on December 4, 1910, at Eliza's homeplace near McLain. The local newspaper ran an article about the wedding titled "Notes from McLain: The Greene-Roberts Wedding." (It is not uncommon to find our family's last name misspelled—with an "e" —as we live in a county named Greene.) The article shared that the happy couple received as wedding gifts "twenty pounds of rice, several old shoes and several other presents that space forbids us to mention. . . ."[2]

By the time Eliza and he married, Jake was already serving as a Deputy Sheriff for the Greene County Sheriff's Department. Besides his work in law enforcement, Jake was also a farmer.

The couple started their family a little over a year after they married, on January 11, 1912, with the birth of a daughter, Alise Bernell. 1912 was also a momentous year as Jake began his term as Greene County's youngest sheriff at twenty-eight. Around this time, he acquired the property in Leakesville and also purchased land near the Clarks Chapel Community on the Chickasawhay River. Jake purchased the house property in 1914 and built a beautiful home for his family in Leakesville, where the three of them would live. The house was near Main Street and the courthouse where Jake would fulfill his term as sheriff.

Jake and Eliza's first child, daughter Bernell

My grandparents' first son, Jacob Francis, was born on November 12, 1914, and named after his father. Their youngest son, William Lafayette, arrived thirteen months later, on December 31, 1915. Only thirteen months apart, Jacob and William were about the same size and had similar features, making them look more like twins. The Jake Green family was now complete with three precious children. Jake was busy farming and seeking out his law enforcement career, and Eliza took care

Jake's forever home he built for Eliza

of the home and reared the children. The two were also active Leakesville United Methodist Church members and participated in various community events.

Over the next few years, the children quickly grew. The older son, Jacob, who later became my father, and his younger brother, William, loved the outdoors and playing around any water source they could find. Due to their playful habits of playing in the muddy waters of the Chickasawhay River and the branch of the river not far from their house, Jake's sons received nicknames related to their favorite water creatures—Polliwogs and Wiggle Tails, common names for tadpoles. The boys would often bring home their watery treasures in whatever vessel they could find. Jake and Eliza adopted the words as pet names for their boys. Over time, Polliwog became Polly, and Wiggle lost his "Tail." Those nicknames stuck with my daddy and my uncle until they died. Most people never knew their given names and only knew the two Green brothers as Polly and Wiggle.

The Greens were a precious little family of five, living and loving the simple life found in Leakesville and enjoying their property on the

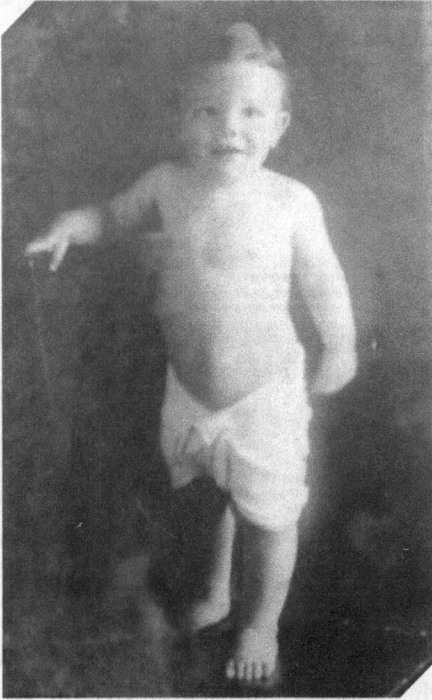

My father, Polly,
as a Toddler

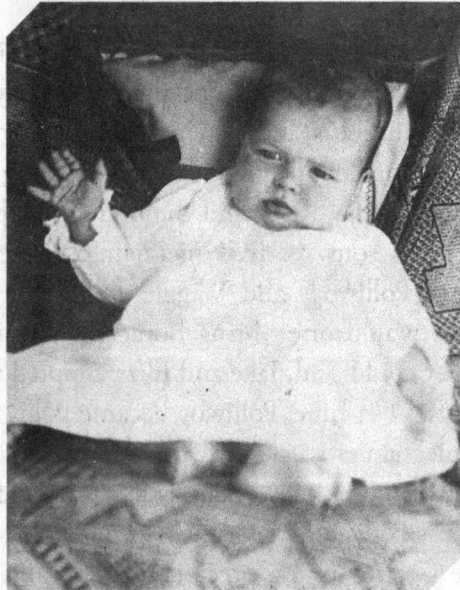

My uncle, Wiggle,
as a young boy

Chickasawhay River that Jake had acquired. The camp on the river became one of the family's favorite spots to spend time away. Bernell, Polly, and Wiggle so adored and admired their father. Jake's children seldom saw him without a badge on his shirt, wearing his favorite hat, and a particular gun on his side. Church, family, community, and friends constituted a good life, and Jake and his family were soaking up every minute of it.

Neither husband nor wife could imagine the horror that would soon shatter their lives forever.

Never to be the same again.

CHAPTER TWO

"The Wettest Dry State"

P ROHIBITION began as a well-intentioned and earnest effort by politicians and temperance movement leaders to stem the tide of evils threatening Americans due to the overuse of alcohol. However, none could have envisioned how differently and disastrously the period would end. Former President Herbert Hoover referred to Prohibition as "the great social and economic experiment." A sharp contrast soon appeared between the good intentions inspiring these thirteen years and the rise of the very criminal acts that the Volstead Act sought to curtail.

Mississippi outlawed alcohol in 1908, a decade before the passage of the Eighteenth Amendment. Mississippi Governor Edmund F. Noel stated in 1908, "If I were called upon to name one thing that wrought the most harm in the world, caused more poverty, heartaches, blighted lives, frustrated ambition, than all other agencies for evil combined, I should say the intemperate use of intoxicating liquors . . ."[1] and, as of January 1909, all liquor licenses were considered null and void. The new law that prohibited alcohol production, sale, and distribution divided Mississippians into two sides of the Prohibition Coin: Heads up for faith, family, and morality, and Tails up for money, politics, and immorality. It began tearing apart Mississippi, its counties, and its residents. It sounds crazy, but the state of Mississippi put a tax on liquor sales, despite passing a law not to sell it in any form. The tax was labeled the "Black Market Tax." In Jackson, one could find a vehicle parked outside the Capitol and its occupants selling liquor. In Mississippi, it was evident that Prohibitionists had the law they wanted, the people had their liquor, and the State had its taxes. Thus, the nickname given to Mississippi during that era was "the wettest dry state."[2]

In January of 1919, the rest of America joined Mississippi as two-thirds of America's state legislatures approved the Eighteenth Amendment, banning liquor manufacturing, selling, and distribution. The National Prohibition Act, otherwise known as the Volstead Act, endured a difficult beginning, including a congressional override of Woodrow Wilson's presidential veto.[3] Named for Andrew Volstead, the Minnesota Representative who championed the bill's passage, the federal legislation ushered in the era of American history known as Prohibition on January 16, 1920.[4] The language of the National Prohibition Act gave chief authority for enforcement to the Internal Revenue Service (IRS), a division of the U.S. Treasury Department.

"SEC. 5. The Commissioner of Internal Revenue, his assistants, agents, and inspectors, and all other officers of the United States whose duty it is to enforce criminal laws, shall have all the power for the enforcement of the War Prohibition Act or any provisions thereof which is conferred by law for the enforcement of existing laws relating to the manufacture or sale of intoxicating liquors under the laws of the United States."[5]

The IRS established the Prohibition Unit on December 22, 1919,[6] and appropriated funds to hire 1,500 agents throughout the country.[7] The annual salary for these positions fell in a range between $1,200 to $3,000.[8] Only a little, if any, training was required, not even the Civil Service Exam. This open-ended policy left the door open for Congressmen and local agencies to appoint whomever they chose. Once selected, these agents were issued a gun, given little formal training, and told to get the job done—investigating, detecting, and punishing those who broke any of the alcohol laws.

Oddly enough, historical information on the U.S. Marshal's website lists their agency as "the principal enforcing agents of the Prohibition

Laws until the Treasury Department created the Bureau of Prohibition in 1927."[9] Despite notation discrepancies, personnel of the IRS and the U.S. Marshals worked well together in enforcing Prohibition laws in Mississippi and especially in the Piney Woods region. Several other federal agencies, including the U.S. Postal Service, the Federal Bureau of Investigation, and U.S. Customs, would work in concert to maintain law and order in a supposedly dry country.[10]

The Prohibition Unit of the Internal Revenue Service would eventually morph into what is today the Bureau of Alcohol, Tobacco, Firearms and Explosives. My grandfather was "one of 95 agents ATF lost between January 17, 1920, and December 5, 1933."[11] Mississippi played a unique role in the Prohibition saga, and Jake was a prominent figure in the storyline. The nation's twentieth state passed a statewide prohibition law in 1908, twelve years before federal Prohibition was enacted.[12] On January 7, 1918, Mississippi was the first state to ratify the Eighteenth Amendment. Oddly enough, the Magnolia State would not pass a law outlawing Prohibition until 1966 and became the last state in the nation to do so.[13] However, citizens of every county in Mississippi would not be granted the ability to possess alcohol legally until July 2, 2020[14], which went into effect on January 1, 2021.

On December 5, 1933, after thirteen years of National Prohibition, the voting into law of the Twenty-First Amendment repealed the Eighteenth Amendment and ended the battle of Prohibition nationally. Thirty-three more years of Prohibition continued in Mississippi before residents of each county would be able to vote to be wet or dry.

Mississippi judge and legislator Soggy Sweat is known for his speech on the legalization of whiskey in the early 1950s.[15] Sweat presented both sides of the argument by answering the question of how he felt about whiskey, "If when you say 'whiskey' you mean the devil's brew, the poison scourge, the bloody monster, that defiles innocence, dethrones reason, destroys the home, creates misery and poverty, yea, takes the bread from the mouths of little children . . . then certainly I am against it,"[16] Sweat began, and then flipped the coin. "But if when you say 'whiskey' you mean the oil of conversation, the philosophic wine, the ale that is consumed when good fellows get together, that puts a song in their hearts and laughter on their lips . . . if you mean that drink, the sale of which pours into our treasuries untold millions of dollars . . . then certainly I am for it," he says.[17]

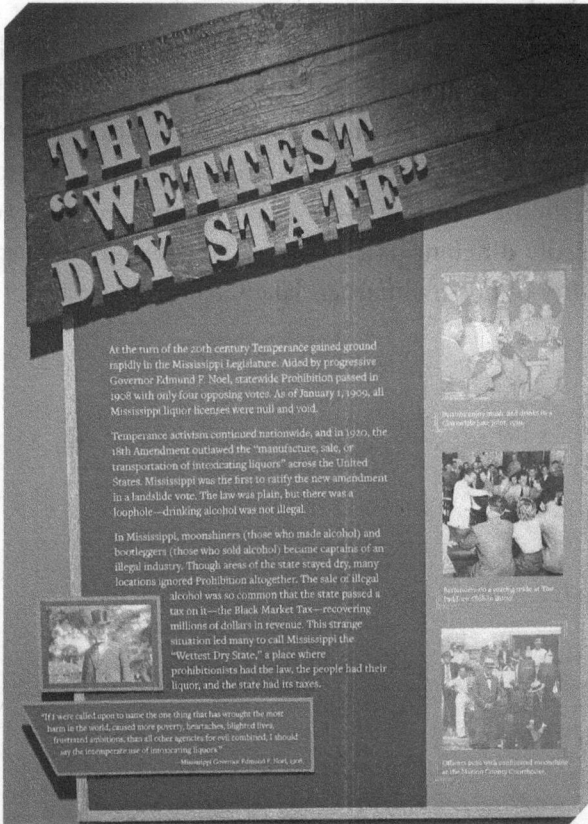

Segment of 2021 Prohibition Exhibit at Mississippi Museum of History

Since Prohibition started in 1920, Greene County had often been called one of Mississippi's wettest "dry" counties. Residents who chose not to consume liquor were outnumbered 3 to 1 as the results came into the Greene County Courthouse in 2012 from across the county.[18] The poll results would cause future consequences that worldly conformers could not even imagine. Making distribution legal in the county did not make it right morally, but consumers felt better about their choices.

Mississippians will always find two sides to most coins, and prohibition is not exempted from the coin toss. Due to liquor manufacture and distribution, countless lives were lost on both sides of the lawless coin.

That is a fact and not an opinion.

Useless deaths.

The evils of the Prohibition period loomed larger than life for two south Mississippi families. Jacob "Jake" Francis Green and Lawrence Dunnam were gunned down on April Fool's Day of 1921 when attempting to shut down an illegal moonshine still and arrest its operators. From that day on, the trajectory of the lives of members of these two families took a markedly different path. This is the convoluted backdrop upon which the story of my grandfather, Jake Green, is staged.

CHAPTER THREE

Jake's Career: Local to Federal

J AKE Green stepped into the law enforcement arena when he became
desk clerk for Sheriff Dan McLeod in 1908. He felt right at home,
being one of the good guys and upholding the laws of Greene County
and the State of Mississippi. Standing behind the badge is where he
wanted to be. From the start, it was his passion to keep his community
safe and to encourage citizens to follow the law.

In 1911, he put his name on the Sheriff of Greene County ballot. He
would go against Webb Walley in the race for sheriff. After the votes were
tallied, Jake came out on top and would begin his term at age twenty-
eight as the county's youngest sheriff. Jake's tenure lasted four years, and
then he decided to look at other occupational options. Webb Walley,
his opponent from the previous election, was voted in and became the
county's new sheriff. As Jake's heart didn't stray too far from a badge-
wearing position, he ran a second time for sheriff but was defeated.
After this, he set his goal at a higher level than the county government.
Enforcement of the Volstead Act of 1919 would not be easy, but several
of Jake's friends felt he was destined to fill one of the positions available
in January of 1920.

In late 1919, Jake's friend, District Attorney Martin Miller, spear-
headed the attempt to have Jake fill one of the inaugural spots on the
team of prohibition officers. He wrote several letters to anyone he knew
could make that appointment come to fruition. He would send Jake

Jake with staff and workers – 1914

copies of the letters to keep him informed of the progress. Jake received this letter from Martin.[1]

> Meridian, Miss.
> December 12th, 1919.

D. J. Gantt, Supervisor & Director,
Federal Prohibition, P. O. Bldg.,
Atlanta, Ga.

Dear Sir: -
  I am very much interested in the enforcement of the Prohibition Laws in Mississippi. The Judicial District of which I am District Attorney, is composed of four counties. Quite a number of stills are located in these counties.

*I have a friend, J. F. Greene of Leakesville, Miss., who has
served his county as sheriff. Mr. Greene made one of the best sheriffs
this state ever had. He is active, intelligent, courageous, shrewd and
a tireless worker. I would like to see Mr. Greene appointed in the
work of enforcing the prohibition laws in our state.*

*Will you kindly advise me as to how many men you will appoint
in Mississippi and what their work will consist of and the salary
attached to the position.*

*If Mr. Greene applys [applies] for the position with you, I am
sure that you will make no mistake if you appoint him, Besides all
of the above good qualities, Mr. Greene is absolutely dependable.*

Thanking you for this information, I am,
Very truly yours,

MVBM-H

Six days later, Miller received this reply from the Atlanta office of the
Prohibition unit.[2]

Atlanta, Ga.,
December 18, 1919.

Copy.

Hon. Martin Miller,
Meridian, Miss.

Sir: -
    *Your letter of the 12th instant has been received, in the interest
of the appointment of Mr. J. F. Greene, to a position as Federal
Prohibition Agent in the State of Mississippi.*
    *At the beginning there will be only eight Prohibition agents
appointed in Mississippi, and the compensation at the outset will
be $1500.00 per annum plus the statutory increase of $240.00 per*

annum, and all actual and necessary expenses when absent from home.

I am transmitting your letter to Mr. Calvin Wells, for consideration and have requested him to look into the qualifications of Mr. Greene.

Respectfully,

D. J. Gantt,
Supervising Fed. Pro. Agent.

Miller then penned this letter to Jake.[3]

Meridian, Miss.,
December 20th, 1919.

Mr. J. F. Greene,
Leakesville,
Miss.

Dear Jake: -
I am enclosing you a copy of letter from Gantt to me. If you want a position with these people, I hope we will be able to land you one.

Jake, it has been something like seven Christmases since I had the pleasure of meeting you. During this time, you certainly have done many acts of kindness for me. It is not often that one meets and knows a fellow that is capable of being as true and loyal a friend as you have been. Every year that has gone by has strengthened our friendship and made it more pleasant to us. It is friendships like this that go so far to make life happy and to smooth out the rough places along its pathway. I have, since first knowing you, counted you one of my best and truest friends. In this, I have never been disappointed, and hope as the years go by that this valuable friendship will grow stronger and better.

I take this opportunity of expressing my wish for you a most
happy Xmas and a very pleasant new year, I am,

Your friend,
Martin Miller

Although the process seemed slow at times, Martin Miller's consistent efforts to reach out to Mississippi's Congressional Representative, Byron Patton "Pat" Harrison, in Washington yielded results. Prior to serving in the legislature, Harrison and his wife—a Leakesville native—resided in her hometown and were prominent members of the community. Harrison served in the Mississippi Legislature from 1911 until 1919. That same year, he continued representing his home state of Mississippi as a United States Senator until his death in 1941.

After several months of persuasive actions by very influential individuals, Christmas came early for Jake as he was among the country's first prohibition agents hired to enforce the Volstead Act. He was assigned to the Southern District of the Gulf Department in Mississippi. He was labeled a Special Agent for the Treasury Department, Office of the Secretary, and was considered a United States Marshal. The annual salary would be around $1,500. He did get a small stipend for a few items needed. It was not the salary that attracted Jake to the position but the job of protecting his family, town, county, state, and country from the dreaded liquor manufacturing and distribution.

With District Attorney Martin Miller and Congressman Pat Harrison's support and endorsement, Jake began his obligated duty on January 17, 1920. The job took him all over south Mississippi and kept him away from home for long periods. He kept in touch with Eliza and the children through letters, postcards, and occasional phone calls. The family, especially Eliza, missed him tremendously, but they knew he was doing something he felt so strongly about. The danger of the position had Eliza try to convince Jake to quit and come home and find a local occupation where he wouldn't be gone so much or be in such a dangerous position. She supported him but so wanted him home with her and the children.

Special Agent Jake Green

Jake's IRS Special Agent Badge

The couple soaked up the time they had when he could break away from work and visit home between job assignments. In one of their last conversations, Jake promised Eliza he would grant her request to find other work as soon as he could work out the logistics.

Although he discussed his upcoming resignation with fellow officers, it would be a little too late for what would transpire.

CHAPTER FOUR

CHAPTER FOUR

The Piney Woods Creek Murders

AFTER fourteen months of service as a Special Agent with the U.S. Treasury Department, Jake felt secure in his new position. He was very confident in his dealings with local moonshiners. One day in late March of 1921, active moonshiner Sid Baggett from Sumrall, Mississippi, approached Jake with some very interesting information he said might assist in a future raid. He provided Jake with a detailed map of the specific location of an operational whiskey still on Piney Woods Creek, in the northwest corner of Greene County near the Perry County line. The still was owned by Henry Bond, who lived in the nearby neighborhood close to the location drawn on the map. The still site was along the banks of Piney Woods Creek between Richton and Sand Hill, just over the Perry County Line into Greene County.

Baggett's carefully-drawn map showed Jake how to get to the site. It was in a swampy area surrounded by dense trees and bushes. One would have to walk in from any direction because it was so overgrown. Rumor had it that Bond's Still had been up and running for approximately six weeks before the day of the raid. Bond and Baggett competed in southern Mississippi for customers wanting the best shiny around. Could Baggett have possibly double-crossed Green, giving the bootleggers a heads-up that the Prohibition agent would be coming their way? Some answers may never be known.

After being away from home for almost two weeks on official business, Jake arrived in Hattiesburg, fifty miles west of Leakesville. He would contemplate his best plan for catching the bootleggers the next day. On Thursday, Jake wrote a postcard to Eliza and mailed it on the same day—March 31, 1921. His words seem to foreshadow the events that were to come, "I will go to Richton tomorrow and home Saturday. If I get through in time may come home Friday night."[1]

The last postcard Jake wrote to Eliza the day before his death

Green had arranged for assistance from Lawrence Dunnam, Richton's Town Marshal. Dunnam was also a Deputy Sheriff for Greene County and was familiar with the local moonshiners. Weeks earlier, Dunnam had served papers for the Greene County Sheriff's Department and picked up Johnny Adams and one of Henry Bond's sons, Ernest. The apple, it seemed, had not fallen far from the tree when it came to the Bond Family and a jug of moonshine. Bond's partners in the moonshine business—Mancy Kelly, Johnny Adams, and Will Morris—lived in the area adjacent to the site. Each man had his interests in the manufacturing and distribution of toxic shiny.

Officers Green and Dunnam knew each other on more than a business level. They were distant cousins, both having Greene County roots. When Baggett relayed the tip to Green, Jake knew Dunnam would be the best man to assist him in the raid on Bond's Still. The two officers did not want anyone to tip off the moonshiners that they were headed that way. So, they arranged for a Mr. Rogers, a local taxi driver from McLain, Mississippi, to drop them off about a mile from the proposed site and wait for them to return. The officers advised Rogers to go for help if they did not return to the car within a reasonable period. The driver then dropped off the two officers on the outskirts of Piney Woods Creek, approximately six miles out of Richton. As Rogers watched the men head off down the old road, he settled into his taxi to wait for them to return.

As the officers put more distance between themselves and the drop-off point, they could hear voices and knew they were most likely in the correct area of the swampland. Weaving their way through the tangled underbrush, Green and Dunnam both cautiously approached as they moved closer to the location marked "X" on the map. Both men listened as the moonshiners proclaimed, as they worked on the still, that because Sid Baggett had treated them so dirty, they would not be surprised if Jake Green came in to catch them. Bond also boasted to his bootlegger buddies that he, in no way, would give up his shiny.

The officers split up, each man planning to appear on opposite sides of the still. By this time, the moonshiners had fired up the still and tested its results.

Stepping into view, Green yelled, "Hands Up!"

Gunfire immediately started between the officers and the moonshiners.

Dunnam and Kelly exchanged gunfire. Each caused damage to the other.

Green used one pistol shot to strike Bond in the stomach area. The bullet went almost through his torso. Bond went down, and Green then exchanged shots with Adams.

Suddenly, Bond raised himself to a sitting position, at close range to Green, and used his shotgun to send blasts of buckshot directly down Green's pistol muzzle. Several pellets hit Green's thumb as he gripped the gun's handle. Several more pieces of shot hit Green in the face; others struck the muzzle of his weapon. Worst of all, the primary blast from Bond's shotgun blew the top of Green's head off. Green died immediately from that blast.

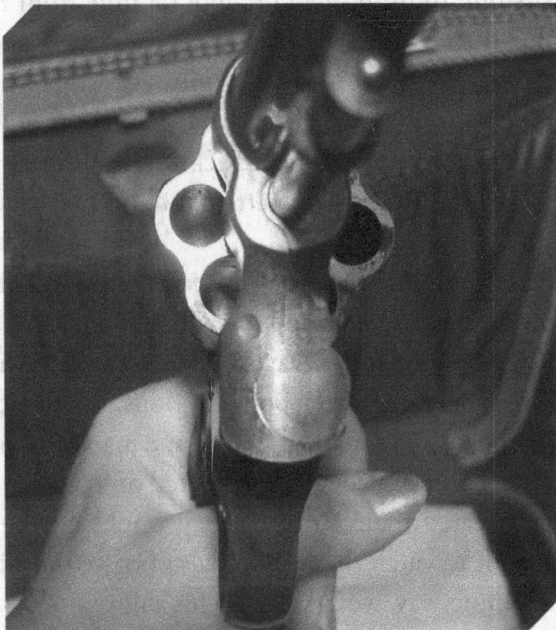

Notches from buckshot the day Jake died

After being shot by Dunnam, Kelly stood up but left his mangled shotgun where he had fallen. Part of the gunstock had been shot off in the gun battle, although the weapon was still in useable condition.

Officer Dunnam bravely continued to hold his ground against the remaining moonshiners. A shot to his chest hurled him down on his elbows and knees. Bond and Kelly were leaving the scene when they saw Adams take the shotgun Kelly had left behind on the ground and use four shotgun blasts to rip into the marshal's back as Dunnam pled for his life. Dunnam was shown no mercy, with Green now lying dead on the other side of the still site.

Now that the moonshiners had eliminated both officers, Kelly retrieved his shotgun from Adams. The moonshiners fled into the deep woods and returned to their homes in the nearby neighborhood.

Would anyone find out that they were murderers?

Only time would tell.

CHAPTER FIVE

The Manhunt

AFTER hearing less than a minute of gunfire, Rogers waited for the officers to return to his taxi. When they did not, he went to the closest house and called Richton authorities to tell them what he knew about the officers' plans. Several carloads of citizens left Richton for the scene around 2:30 P.M. with guns loaded and ready. Although unsure of where to search, they knew the closest proximity, as Rogers had shared where he dropped the officers off. After a two-hour search around Piney Woods Creek, searchers located the shattered bodies of the two slain officers lying lifeless on opposite sides of the whiskey still. Green's pistol was beside him, and Dunnam was still clutching his handgun in one hand.

This heartbreaking account of what searchers discovered was reported in an article, "Double Tragedy Marks Still Raid," which ran in the *Greene County Herald* a week after the murders.

". . . His [the taxi driver's] report stirred the town of Richton into prompt action and soon a posse went to the scene of the killing and recovered the bodies of the dead officers which were carried to Richton.

The top of Jake's head had been blown off with a load of buck-shot and he had fallen dead on his face, likely instantly killed. His pistol showed all balls except one which had been snapped emptied and some shot fouled the chamber of his pistol indicating that the fire which killed him was directed up his pistol barrel.

Dunnam had a large hole blown in his breast a wound in his arm and other wounds indicating that he had been badly shot up and by shot-gun."[1]

Perry County Sheriff Dennis and his officers and Greene County Sheriff Webb Walley gathered evidence until sunset on that deadly Friday afternoon. The group collected multiple articles of evidence at the site, including several quarts of shiny liquor, one of which they found hidden inside a hat belonging to Adams.

Next, authorities searched for and found Kelly with a bullet wound to his arm at his home. He stated that he had snagged himself on a fence line.[2] In his home, officers found a gun with a mangled stock that matched broken parts of the same gun found near the crime scene. When located, Adams had a gunshot wound in his hand. A search of Bond's home uncovered his gun and a bloody shot sack.[3]

One of the early heroes of the investigation was Richton physician R. A. Cochran.[4] Sometime that afternoon, within hours of the murders, he had been summoned to make a house call for an injury. That patient would turn out to be Henry Bond. Bond had a "bullet hole through his body in the region of one of the lungs."[5] Cochran's instincts immediately went into high gear when this man, whom he did not know, gave a flimsy excuse that did not match the severity of his wounds.[6] The good doctor found a friend of Bond's with him, William Morris. Knowing his patient needed more care than he could provide, Cochran transported the two—Bond and Morris—to his office in the town of Richton.

When the trio arrived, Cochran's office staff quickly informed him of the news of the gruesome murders. Immediately, many of the dots of Dr. Cochran's suspicions lined up as alarm bells inside him clanged louder and louder. Stepping out of the exam room in his office, Cochran found a phone in a quiet office and bravely called authorities. Not long after, law enforcement officers arrived and arrested Morris as an accomplice.

Although he had left the still before Green and Dunnam had arrived, William Morris was indirectly involved as a partner in the moonshine productions and was now considered the fourth member of the ruthless crew of moonshiners turned murderers. While in the custody of Constable O. E. Carter, Morris confessed as he was being transported to the jail in Hattiesburg.[7] He said that "Bond, Adams, Kelly and himself were the only ones implicated in the shooting and that Adams did the shooting, which resulted in the deaths of the two officers."[8]

W. D. Mills, Justice of the Peace, was the officer to accompany Bond to Laurel.[9] As the larger town was almost fifty miles northwest of Richton, the train was the fastest mode of transportation. While waiting in Dr. Cochran's office for about a half hour, Bond rambled on, talking incessantly, his wounds having sent him into a state of semi-consciousness.[10] Despite his struggle to remain awake, Bond still stuck to the same story he had told to Dr. Cochran, that while "shooting craps" in the woods, he was struck "by a stray bullet."[11] Initial press reports gave the moonshiner a limited chance for a full recovery.[12] Bond would remain in the Laurel Hospital for a few weeks, lingering between life and death.

Adams and Kelly were also arrested by nightfall, the same day as the murders, and taken to the jail in Richton. Several threats to the moonshiners' lives began to cause an uproar. Later that evening, they were transported to the Hattiesburg Jail for safekeeping. Bond was in Laurel's South Mississippi Charity Hospital, not expected to live, and unwilling to talk about his part in the murders.[13]

Four days later, on Tuesday, April 5, S.S. "Sid" Baggett, the fifth and last moonshiner associated with the Piney Woods Creek murders, was arrested and transported to Jackson, where he would remain in the Hinds County jail for his safety.[14]

These words from an article appearing in *The Times-Picayune* newspaper best sum up the futility and senselessness of these heinous murders,

> "Just what happened in the thickly grown swamp where the pair
> of raiders worked their way through the mire and entangling
> vines may never be clearly established . . .

Indications were that the raiders were shot down and then to make sure they would tell no tales the moonshiners went up to them and deliberately pumped bullets into them as they lay wounded and helpless on the ground."[15]

From the moment that news of the murders first reached the ears of local authorities, a certain and determined group of local, state, and federal law enforcement officials immediately merged, making it their mission to do all in their power to bring the killers of Jake Green and Lawrence Dunnam to justice.

CHAPTER SIX

Laid to Rest

B Y late afternoon on that terrible April Fool's Day, John B. Browder and his son, Edward, driving a mule and buggy, were sent into the deep woods to retrieve the bodies. They brought the bullet-riddled corpses out to the main road, where a truck was waiting to carry both officers to the home of Lawrence Dunnam in Richton. Green's body remained at the Dunnam home while authorities waited for instructions from his family.

On the evening of Friday, April 1, word arrived that Jake's family was requesting that his body be brought home to Leakesville. The Green family was devastated at the news of Jake's death, as only a few months earlier, they had lost Jake's father to pneumonia. Before midnight, my Granddaddy Green was delivered to his residence for the last time, and grieving family members began preparing for the burial that would take place on Saturday, April 2.

One of six deputies in Mississippi's Southern District for the U.S. Marshal's Service had these glowing words to share about my granddaddy:

"Greene was sheriff of Greene c[C]ounty, and was a fearless officer, much feared by law-breakers in his own and adjoining counties, . . . and has been one of the best, most active and fearless of all the national prohibition officers in this state.

I have arrested a number of Volstead act violators with his assistance, and he was ever ready to aid all officers of the law. He was as game a man as I ever saw—absolutely without fear. All officers of south Mississippi will feel deep regret at his death, and we all feel that the law-abiding people have lost a brave and efficient officer, while his brother officers have lost a friend and a valuable aid in their work.[1]

Loposser went on to share his admiration for Marshal Dunnam.

"I also knew Marshal Dunham well: he was also a brave man and fine officer and the people of his county and town will miss his valuable services. He is the second marshal of Richton killed in performance of duty. Marshal Milstead, of Richton, was killed last year in trying to keep the peace when a gang of rowdies took the town."[2]

These words, contained in an article about the Piney Woods Creek murders one week after the event, perhaps summed up best the honor and integrity of the character of officers Jake Green and Lawrence Dunnam and testified to their dedication to protecting their community and upholding the law at all costs,

"Who can gauge the anguish of the sorrow, stricken hearts of the families of these dead men, whose lives were snuffed out while in the discharge of their sworn duty of the law to help put down a nefarious and outlawed traffic by both federal and state laws. Let it be hoped that the fearful sacrifices which they paid will not have proved in vain but that people will wake up to the situation and rally to the need of the hour and in this crisis in turning the tide against the banded and accursed liquor traffic."[3]

Lawrence Dunnam was forty-five years old at the time of his death and survived by a loving wife and many children.[4] The law enforcement officer was well respected in his community, as evidenced by the outpouring of sympathy and the large crowd assembled for his service. *The Richton Dispatch* would report that "Dunnam's funeral was the most impressive ever held in Richton."[5] For two hours, around the time of the services for Richton's Town Marshal on Saturday, April 2, 1921, every business in town locked its doors, and commerce ceased. The Reverends J. L. Low and F. B. Ormond officiated the service held at the Baptist church. Many prominent citizens gave testimonies of Dunnam's honor, integrity, and devotion to his profession; Mayor J. T. Allums offered glowing remarks, as did "J. M. Dees, W. M. Dorsett, Dr. W. D. Mobley," and local attorney A. R. Shoemaker.[6] Dunnam was laid to rest in the Richton city cemetery.

Richton Town Marshal
W. Lawrence Dunnam

Dunnam's grave
marker in the Richton
Town Cemetery

The local newspaper also printed this heartfelt poem submitted by an anonymous friend of Dunnam's.

In Memoriam[7]

"Our town seems deserted without you, dear Lawrence,
The loss can ne'er be repaired;
You were a kind and loving friend,
There was never a better man.

God saw fit to take you
From dear ones kind and true,
To help brighten another world
Where none but the good will do.

It seems so lonesome without you
In the house that you call home.
But may God in His infinite power,
Console us in our dark hour.

We listen for footsteps,
Together we all wait in vain.
For the voice of one we all loved
For one we will never see again.

But together we will hope and pray
For the day that we soar
To a better world than this
Is to you on yonder shore."

—A Friend

My grandfather, Jake, was thirty-seven years old, in the prime of his life when the moonshiner's bullets cut him down. My grandmother, Eliza, was twenty-nine and was now a widow—Jake Green's Widow—and her children were now fatherless. My father, known to all as Polly, was only six years old when he lost his daddy. His older sister Bernell was nine; his younger brother Wiggle was five. Jake's mother, Iddie, was a new widow herself, having lost her husband to pneumonia only months before. Jake's death must have seemed like a dreaded nightmare to his grief-stricken family, one that would now continue.

Jake would be laid to rest at the feet of his father, Franklin James Green, in the McLeod Cemetery in Leakesville not far from his home. It was just a field at that time. His father's grave was still a new site, and now Jake was there so close to his father. Mourners placed beautiful white lilies over the mound of dirt covering Jake's grave. Other flowers were all around, given to the family in memory of the life he lived.

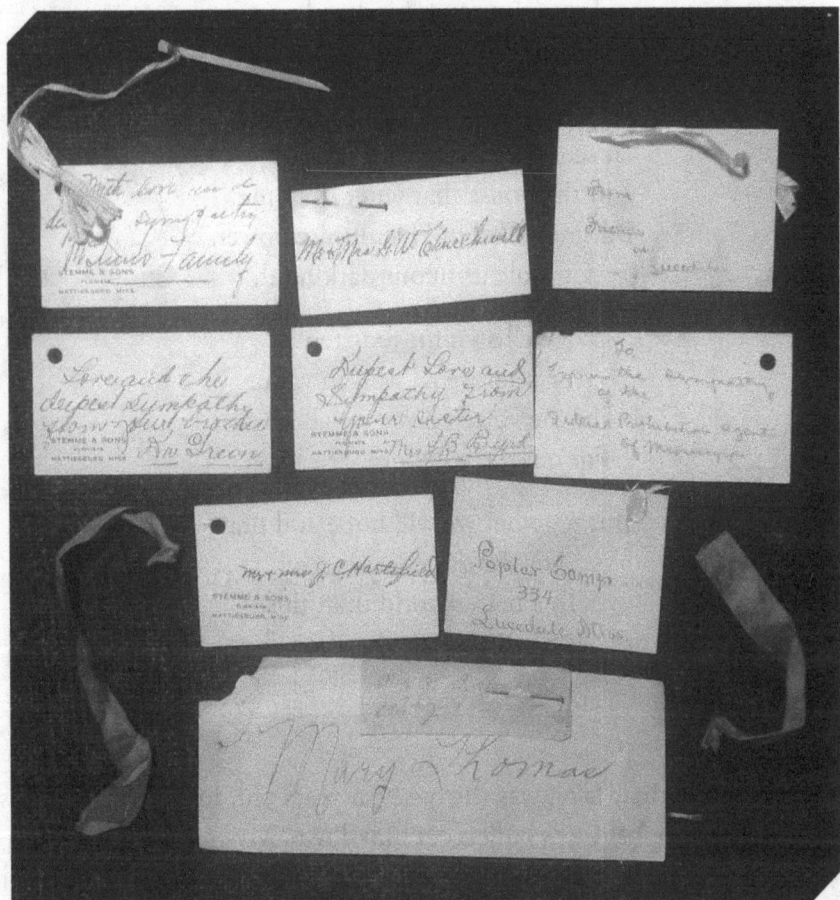

Cards from Jake's funeral flowers

Jake Green's headstone

This poem was written for Jake's mother by Miss Annie Denman, a woman who served as a teacher at the Mississippi Institute for the Blind,[8] where M. L. Batson, Jake's brother-in-law, was the director. The elegy accompanied my grandfather's obituary in the local newspaper.

That Boy of Mine

He gave his life, that boy of mine,
For such a noble cause
To bless our hearts, to keep our homes
And Mississippi's laws.

I scarce can bear to think of him;
But when I would repine,

I see the angels gather round,
That noble boy of mine.

I see the Savior smile on him,
And hear His praise: "Well done."
And then I am happy to have borne,
The land so fair a son.

I'm glad his father didn't have
This agony to bear;
I'm sure his spirit met our son
And bade him welcome there.

I now recall his childish touch
And how he used to play
The little clothes I used to mend.
His very tender way.

His merry words and all he said,
And how his smiles would shine,
Tis then my heart just breaks to see
That little boy of mine.

I'd give a year of life to kiss
Away one childish sore.
To dry his tears by saying "Son,
'Twont hurt you any more."

But words can't span a mother's love
This love is so divine.
I miss him so; but he is great
That darling boy of mine.

Too much death too close in time, and much too much for the Green family to comprehend. One would hope it was all a dream, but as the sun went down on that burial field that dreaded Saturday afternoon, Eliza walked away speechless as she said goodbye to her beloved Jake through tears. Never another "I love you" spoken by her lips. Eliza would need to try to stay strong for the children. However, Bernell, Polly, and Wiggle were now old enough to know their lives would never be the same, the void created that April Fool's Day would never be filled.

As his last postcard to Eliza said, Jake made it home that Friday night, except without a breath of life.

Jake returned to his Forever Love for the last time.

CHAPTER SEVEN

Birth of the Green Widow

ELIZA Ellen Roberts Green became the Green Widow that April Fools' morning in 1921, the instant that Jake took his last breath and fell to his death from the aim of Henry Bond's gun. Bitterness deep within her soul would become the norm, where love and laughter once reigned. Sympathy condolences abounded in person and through telegraphs, letters, and phone calls. Although Eliza did appreciate each expression of comfort, nothing would bring her beloved Jake back to her and their children. Eliza's once sweet, affectionate, and supple personality died that awful day. In its place emerged the persona of the Green Widow: bitter, angry, hopeless, independent, dominant, and mostly heartbroken. Life, as it was, would never be the same again.

Shortly after Jake's death, my grandmother, whom we called Mimi, filed a "claim for compensation"[1] as she was now a survivor of a fallen federal officer. In a letter dated May 4, 1921, the United States Employees' Compensation Commission informed Mimi that her claim had been "approved and an award of $35 per month made to you so long as you remain unmarried. This award represents the maximum amount that can be allowed under the law."[2]

Enclosed with the letter were several items. First, a check covering the period between April 2 and 30, 1921, was included. Second, an ample "supply of forms to be used in claiming further compensation."[3] According to instructions in the letter, she was to file claims four times a year—January, April, July, and October. As far as I know, these federal compensation checks were paid to my grandmother throughout her life, providing a financial supplement to care for her children.

In a related letter written to Mimi on July 12, 1921, Ellis Chapman wrote to inform her that he had forwarded "an itemized receipted bill for the burial expenses of Jake"[4] to D. J. Gantt, the Supervising Federal Prohibition Agent in Atlanta, Georgia. Chapman was the Federal Prohibition Agent in Charge of the Gulf Department of the Treasury Department and, as such, headed up the agency's operations in Mississippi. He would play a critical role in investigating Granddaddy Green's murder.

In the letter, Chapman wrote, as had so many in letters written to my grandmother, about how much the friendship he shared with Jake had meant to him:

> "You said in your letter that you was glad that some one
> thought of you all, I will say that there is never a day that passes
> that I do not think of you and those dear little children for
> there is things in this office that I see every day that reminds
> me of my dear friend Jake and naturally I will think of you all
> and oftin [often] wish that there was some-thing that I could do
> to make you [your] grief easier to bear. You said that if it were
> not for your little children that Death would be sweet to you,
> of-course I can not [cannot] realize or appreciate your suffering
> but, I do not think that you should feel that way, for you know
> not what is stored in the future for you, and possible when
> those little fellows grows larger they will be so much company
> and your interest in them will be so great that you will forget to
> some extent, the sad past."[5]

A once smiling, happy, fun-loving wife and mother, she started the journey with her new title: Jake Green's Widow, the Widow Green, and the Green Widow. Just plain "Widow" is what many family members called her, including my father, Polly. He addressed her by this title more times than not. He occasionally called her Momma when he got up the

Eliza with her three children: Bernell (standing center), Polly (standing right), and Wiggle (seated)

nerve to question her authority, which was not very often. Authority was one of the Green Widow's dominant traits. She lived it and demanded her way of doing things of all who were part of her "web." My grandmother would be known by this persona—the Green Widow—for the remainder of her life. Even after her death, many of her spiderlings shared her bitterness and held on to it, while others chose happiness. However, for most of us, the anger occasionally found its way in.

Eliza's Little Gentlemen

Jake's sons growing up

Eliza on the front porch in the years after Jake's death

As adulthood approached each of them, Polly stayed closest to "Widow" as he lived across the street with his wife and family. Wiggle moved an hour away, and Bernell was back and forth but always lived close to Wiggle's residence on First Terrace Street in Hattiesburg. For most of her childhood, Joy, Bernell's daughter, lived with the Green Widow. Bernell and Joy were considered residents of Leakesville from 1939 through the late 1940s. Bernell went to work at a shipyard in Biloxi, Mississippi, until World War II was over, and she left Joy with Mimi during that time. Then, Bernell and her daughter moved to Hattiesburg when Joy was in the second grade. She stayed with Mimi every summer while

Bernell was working in Hattiesburg, at least until Joy was old enough to be left alone.

Mimi's house would not hold many happy memories for my cousin. Never were any "I love you" exchanges made between the survivors of Jake Green and his widow. After Jake's murder, Eliza sowed seeds of resentment within her children's broken hearts. Resentment that crippled her over losing her husband so suddenly. Resentment about having to rear three small children as a single mother. Resentment that Bernell, Polly, and Wiggle would now have to grow up without their father's presence, love, and guidance in their lives. Whether they chose to be bitter or better was a decision each of Jake's children would have to make alone.

Mimi as she grew older

Upon my grandfather's death, a pall of silence draped itself over the Jake Green family, which would continue to stifle communication and understanding for generations. Mimi's refusal to allow others into the deep wound within her soul and to look for joy amid deep sorrow, in turn, wounded us all. These words, taken from the novel, *Five Quarters of the Orange* by Joanne Harris, aptly describe my grandmother's transformation on that terrible day, "To her, those petty rules mattered because those were the things she used to control her world. Take them away and she was like the rest of us, orphaned and lost."

One could say that the spirit of the Green Widow never died.

Even today, a part of that "Mimi spirit" lives within each of us, her offspring.

PART II

Entangled

"Oh, what a tangled web we weave, . . ."

—SIR WALTER SCOTT, "MARMION," 1808

CHAPTER EIGHT

The Investigation

A S one of the men killed in the Piney Woods Creek murders was a federal officer, the case immediately garnered national media attention. Over one hundred articles appeared in at least twenty-four newspapers from as far north as Baltimore, Maryland, as far south as Macon, Georgia, as far east as Richmond, Virginia, and as far west as Denver, Colorado. One of the peculiarities of the various accounts of the case was multiple misspellings of the names of both the deceased and those responsible for their deaths.

The *Greene County Herald* would report in a lengthy article published on April 8, 1921, that the news of the murders of my granddaddy Green and Marshal Dunnam gave to Leakesville "one of the worst, if not the worst shock in its history . . ."[1] The fact that two of Greene and Perry Counties' best and brightest had been killed over a few gallons of home-made brew was incomprehensible.

Mississippi, along with Louisiana, Alabama, and the western portion of the panhandle of Florida, comprised the Tenth Prohibition District.[2] This multi-state region of the southeastern United States was a hotbed for bootleg activity. As Jake had been a Special Agent for the Internal Revenue Service, Treasury Department personnel immediately sprang into action. Representatives of the U.S. Marshal Service would also join the investigative team. Unlike the Internal Revenue Service, the Marshal Service divided Mississippi into Northern and Southern districts.[3]

Leakesville was located within the Southern District of Mississippi, comprised of forty-five of the state's eighty-two counties.

Major W. Calvin Wells served as the Federal Prohibition Director of Mississippi.[4] His initial published statement about the case displayed his great respect for my granddaddy and Mr. Dunnam:

"The murder of J.F. Green, former sheriff, and Marshal Lawrence Dunnam brings forcibly before the people of Mississippi what will inevitably continue to take place unless the public conscience views the enforcement of the prohibition laws in the proper light. If such violations are trivialities then our men should not be compelled to die in the enforcement of such laws. If on the other hand moonshining is properly regarded as a serious violation of the law and directly a result in crime, poverty and sorrow then no moonshine still could exist any material length of time. It is for the people of Mississippi to say by their attitude toward these laws to what extent and how the law should be enforced."[5]

A newspaper article published one week after the murders stated that Wells "would attend Federal court in Aberdeen this week and return by Meridian for a conference with Attorney Miller to push the charges to the limit."[6]

Federal Prohibition Agent in Charge Ellis S. Chapman and Martin Miller, the District Attorney of the Tenth District, headquartered in Meridian, arrived on Saturday, April 2, to begin investigating and gathering evidence around the scene of the crime.[7] Officers J. L. Boyd, A. W. Thompson, Glenn Whitehead, and J. L. Buchanan joined them.[8] For the next few days, the investigation team would examine all evidence gathered by the Greene and Perry County Sheriff's personnel on the day of the murders.[9] Evidence collected included a bloody shot sack and a shotgun found at Bond's home, a shotgun with a broken stock found at Kelly's home, a piece of a fractured stock found at the scene, several quarts of shiny around the still site, a hat belonging to Adams with a quart of moonshine whiskey in it, and various other items around the whiskey still.[10]

Determining what firearms were involved was one of the first questions to answer. The conclusion was that both officers used pistols. Bond used a double-barreled shotgun, Kelly had an automatic shotgun, and Adams had a pistol. After closely examining Green's weapon, evidence showed that he had only fired it once. The shots that had killed him also struck his hand simultaneously as he threw up his pistol. One of the same shotgun blasts that killed him also jammed Green's pistol. All wounds indicated that Green was near the individual who fired the fatal shot to the top of his head. Dunnam had a shotgun blast to his chest and four bullets in his back.

Chapman stated, "It was the most horrible affair I have ever had brought to my notice. After Dunnam was shot down and fell on his elbows and knees, still fighting, four shots were fired into his back."[11] Agent Chapman vigorously stated that he would ensure both state and federal charges were filed against the moonshiners.[12] Will Morris gave the first part of a confession on the night of the murders.[13] Chapman received partial confessions from Adams and Kelly on Saturday, April 2.[14] The medical opinion offered Friday on Bond's wounds gave him only a slight chance to survive, but he beat those odds.[15] By Sunday, April 3, Bond remained in the hospital, still refusing to talk.

Although the three moonshiners had originally been arrested near Richton and probably would have been jailed there, the decision was made to move them to another location. Late in the night of April 1, it quickly became apparent to law enforcement officials that emotions were running high within the citizenry of Leakesville over the cold-blooded murders of Green and Dunnam.[16] On Monday morning, April 4, Kelly, Morris, and Adams were moved out of the area by train from Sanford to Jackson by Forrest County Sheriff E.D. Edmonson and his deputies.[17] Feelings continued to run high against all men involved in the murders. They were safest as far away from Greene County as possible. Bond remained in the Jones County jail until his day in court.

The term *capital crime* did not exist in Mississippi's legal code in 1921.[18] Felonies, as they were called at the time, were those for which the defendant might be sentenced to death or imprisonment in the penitentiary if found guilty. Section 957 of the 1917 Mississippi Code states that, "Every person who shall be convicted of murder shall suffer death, unless the jury rendering the verdict shall fix the punishment at imprisonment for life . . ."[19]

On Wednesday, April 6, S.S. "Sid" Baggett, of Sumrall, arrived at the Hinds County Jail, having been arrested the day before.[20] He was apprehended first in Greene County, then sent to the Hattiesburg jail, and finally escorted to Jackson by Prohibition Agents Chapman and Whitehead. He claimed to have given the alleged moonshiners advance notice that Green might be visiting Piney Woods Creek. Baggett was also charged with supplying the map to Agent Green of the still's whereabouts. He could not have imagined that the "X" he marked on that piece of parchment would quickly change so many lives.

Once again, jealousy over a pint of shiny being sold had ignited a deadly chain of events.

CHAPTER NINE

Pre-Trial Motions

I N May of 1921, less than two months after the murders at Piney Woods Creek, the trials of Mancy Kelly and Henry Bond captured the attention of all the citizens of Greene and Perry counties, if not the entire state of Mississippi and beyond. As evidenced by the many articles printed in various newspapers from as far away as Denver, Colorado, and Washington, D.C., countless people across the country closely followed the story of my grandfather's murder. Selecting jurors for the trials soon proved a dilemma for both Prosecution and Defense.

The wheels of justice moved with lightning speed. The May term of the Circuit Court of Greene County opened on April 25, less than one month after the murders, with the process of selecting jurors for that court session. A *venire facias* was issued, which is "a judicial writ [order] directing the sheriff to summon a specified number of qualified persons to serve as jurors."[1] Each potential juror was summoned to appear between April 25 and May 5.

When court opened on Monday, May 9, 1921, indictments were issued against Henry Bond, Mancy Kelly, John Adams, and Will Morris on charges of murder of both Green and Dunnam and also manufacturing and distribution of intoxicating liquor. The case numbers assigned were as follows:

Case 967 – Murder of Jake Green. The Grand Jury presented that "Mancey F. Kelley, Henry A. Bond, John Adams and Will Morris did "unlawfully, wilfully, feloniously, and of malice aforethought kill and murder one J. F. Greene, a human being."[2]

Case 968 – Murder of Lawrence Dunnam. "State of Mississippi vs Henry Bond, John Adams, Mancey F. Kelley, and Will Morris"[3]

Case 969 – Manufacturing and distribution of intoxicating liquor. The Grand Jury presented that "Will Morris, Mancey F. Kelley, Henry A. Bond, and John Adams" did "unlawfully and feloniously make, manufacture, and distill, spiritous, vinous, malted, fermented and intoxicating liquor."[4]

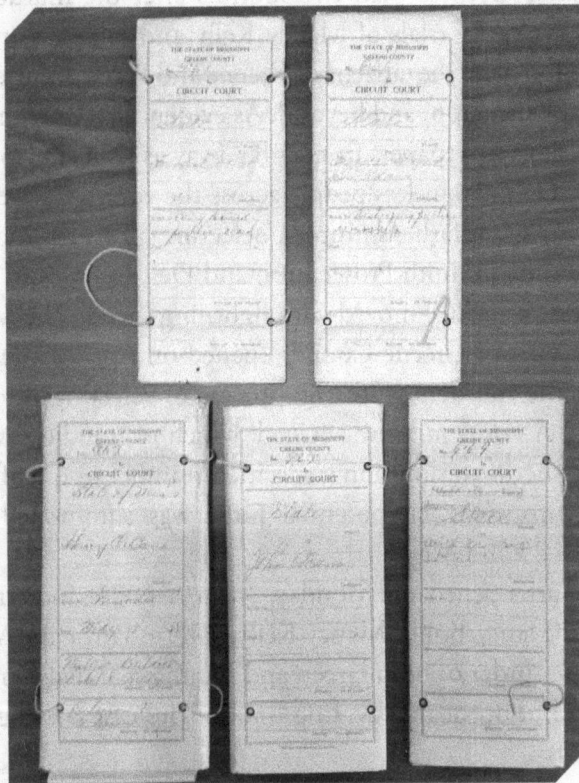

All court case files related to the Piney Woods Creek murders

Another preliminary order of business was the issuance of an *instanter capias*, a court order authorizing an officer of the court to arrest and bring before the court the said person(s) listed in the order.[5]

The State of Mississippi.

To the Sheriff of Greene County—Greeting:
    You are hereby commended to take Will Morris, Mancy
F. Kelley, Henry A. Bond, John Adams, if to be found in
your County, and they safely keep, so that you have their
bodies before the Circuit Court of the County of Greene
in said State, at the Courthouse in the town of Leakesville,
Mississippi, INSTANTER, then and there to answer the State
of Mississippi, on an indictment this day found against them
for distilling liquor.
    And gave there then this writ.

Given under my hand and the seal of said Court, and issued
this the 9 day of May, A.D., 1912 [1921]
John W. Colbert
Clerk of the Circuit Court Greene County, Miss.[6]

The old Greene County Courthouse built in 1899

The current Greene County Courthouse built in 1939

Assigned to represent the State of Mississippi were District Attorneys Martin Miller, E. W. Breland, and E. C. Fishel.[7] Hattiesburg lawyer John R. Tally assisted the prosecution in some cases. The court appointed as defense counsel Cephus A. Anderson and A. E. Anderson to represent Kelly[8], and Marion Reilly and Elmer Busby to represent Bond. The Honorable J.D. Fatheree would preside over the trials.[9]

Indeed, the state's attorneys were hoping for the successful prosecution of the charges against all four men—Adams, Bond, Kelly, and Morris. The common felony charge against them all was murder in the first degree. As this was a capital offense, one could lose one's life if convicted of such a charge. Two options were available for sentencing—life imprisonment or the death penalty. A guilty verdict mandated the death penalty, which in 1921, in Mississippi, meant hanging. Since 1804, this had been the method by which this state had carried out executions.[10] Not until 1940 would the Mississippi Department of Corrections employ another manner of execution—electrocution.[11]

As the court session progressed, people in Leakesville, Richton, and across Mississippi eagerly awaited their copy of the weekly newspaper to discover what transpired at the Greene County Courthouse. Here is a short piece that ran in the *Laurel Daily Leader* on Wednesday, May 11, 1921.

"Richton Moonshine Murderers on Trial"

Leakesville, Miss., May 11.—This little town is rapidly filling with people as the news is made public that the trial of Henry Bond, Mancy Kelly, Jeff Adams and Will Morris, for the murder near Richton of Town Marshal J. Lawrence Dunnam and Prohibition Enforcement Officer Jacob E. Green will be called Wednesday on a petition for a change of venue.

The jail where the four defendants are being held is securely guarded night and day for fear of violence. Dr. Byron Green, brother of one of one of the slain officers, has been here since the opening of the ___ (MISSING WORD) A much larger crowd than the one which has been thronging the town is expected when the trial gets under way.[12]

Once these cases were determined justifiable to try in court, trial dates were set, and jury selection began for each case. When the May session of the Greene County Circuit Court opened on Monday, May 9, jury selection was the first order of business for the upcoming trials of both Mancy Kelly for the murder of Lawrence Dunnam and Henry Bond for the murder of Jake Green.

Mancy Kelly would be tried first. Bond's trial would be second on the court docket, but his jurors were not to be chosen until after Kelly's were confirmed. As Leakesville and Richton, hometowns of officers Green and Dunnam, were small towns near one another, many of those questioned for jury duty had close relationships with Green, Dunnam, or both. As such, it took many days to evaluate the jurors. Attorneys for both Bond and Kelly asked for special *venires* or other groups of citizens from which to select jurors to try the complex cases.[13]

Nine days later, a reporter for the *Laurel Daily Leader* updated coverage of the court's activities. Here is a portion of that article.

"Special Venire for Moonshine Murderers"

. . . A motion for change of venue has been argued pro and con, and denied by the court. A motion for continuance also was denied. Between 300 and 400 people have made the journey to Leakesville, which is not on any main line railroad, to hear the proceedings. Kelly's trial has been set for next Monday, and Thursday is the day set to try Henry Bond, also accused of the crime. Will Morris and Johnny Adams will be tried later.[14]

A special venire to try Kelly was finally empaneled after motions for continuance and change of venue were denied on May 20.

Once the jury selection process had ended, the jury Foreman sent a note to Judge Fatheree:

Honorable J. D. Fatherree, Judge,

We the Grand Jurors for the May 1921 Terms of the
Circuit court of Greene County beg to submit this as our final report.

We have examined 150 witnesses and returned 44 true bills
[a document of actual indictment of a crime]. We feel that if
those who love our state and county should really know the
real conditions in our county brought about by the liquor
traffic, conditions would improve herein immediately., by a
united effort on the part of all true Americans. Greene county
is experiencing its worst crime wave. Under the carpet bag
regeime [regime] we doubt if crime was as rampart [rampant].
Every homicide investigated by this body was directly traceable
to liquor. We have no doubt that more perjury was committed
before the Grand Jury about liquor violations than about all
other crimes combined. Conditions are deploable [deplorable]
in this county and it is going to take the untied [united] efforts
of all good people to improve them. Before this term of court
is over nearly half of the qualified electors of Greene county
will have been called upon to do jury service here. It is as your
honor so clearly and ably charged us: A fight now to see who
will run the country—the shinnie [shiny] makers, their cohorts
and symphathyzers [sympathizers] or law and order. The fight is
far from one [won]. Men of Greene who love the county wake
up and do your part to help win this fight.

We thank the Sheriff and his deputies, the other court
officers for their assistance, to us in our work.

Foreman (signature unreadable)

Smith, Clerk
McLain, Clerk[15]

The families of Granddaddy Green and Marshal Dunnam would not
have to wait much longer. Their day in court was coming.

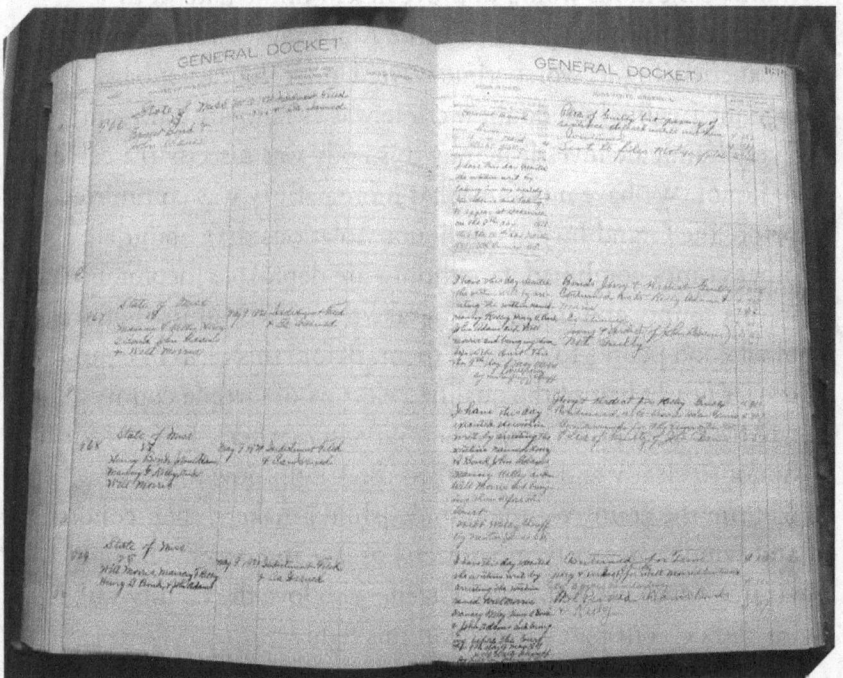

The Greene County Circuit Court Docket Book 1921

INDICTMENT

THE STATE OF MISSISSIPPI, }
Greene   COUNTY } ss.

In the Circuit Court of Greene County, at the May Term,

In the Year of Our Lord Nineteen Hundred and Twenty-one.

The Grand Jury for the State of Mississippi, taken from the body of good and lawful men
of Greene County, in the State of Mississippi, elected, impaneled, sworn and charged to inquire in and for said County, in the State aforesaid, in the name and by the authority of the State of Mississippi, upon their oaths present:

That Mancey F. Kelley, Henry A. Bond, John Adams and Will Morris

in said County, on the _____ day of _____, A. D. 192_1_, did unlawfully, wilfully, feloniously and of malice aforethought kill and murder one J. F. Greene, a human being

contrary to the form of the Statute in such case made and provided, and against the peace and dignity of the State of Mississippi.

M. B. Miller
District Attorney.

Official indictment issued against Kelly, Bond, Adams, and Morris—Case 967

CHAPTER TEN

The Rope's Too Big

MANCY Kelly's trial began on Monday, May 23, 1921, the jury having been selected two days earlier.[1] The charge from Case 968 for the murder of Marshal Lawrence Dunnam was read aloud by the court official after Judge Fatheree, who would preside over all three cases related to the murders of Green and Dunnam, opened the proceedings. As the jury was seated, Kelly's attorneys, Marion W. Reilly and Elmer Busby,[2] immediately began *voir dire* or the process of questioning of witnesses.[3] It would not be until late that afternoon that court would adjourn for the weekend break.

On the afternoon of Monday, May 23, several witnesses were called by the state. The first of these was Frank McKensie, an employee of the Forrest County jail, who had locked up Adams, Kelly, and Morris after their arrival in Hattiesburg.[4] The defense counsel questioned McKensie vigorously, but the jailer remained firm in his testimony. Fellow jailer Forrest County deputy sheriff Joe Gray was summarily interrogated by the defendant's attorneys.[5]

John Adams was the next witness the state called to the stand. Under oath, he made "a full and frank confession" of his part in the murders.[6] Needless to say, as this was incredibly damaging to the defense counsel's case, attorneys for the four men indicted for the Piney Woods Creek murders tried diligently to get Adams to change his testimony under cross examination, but to no avail.

Around four o'clock, District Attorney Martin Miller announced, "the State Rests."[7] Afterward, the defense asked Judge Fatheree for permission to confer with their client, Mancy Kelly, and defense witnesses. The motion was granted, but due to the lengthy conversation that ensued, the judge adjourned the proceedings until the following day.

Tuesday morning found John Adams back in the witness box. Once again, defense counsel tried their best to turn his testimony around but had no more success than they had the day before.

Even though Kelly was the one on trial, the next few witnesses testified regarding Henry Bond, perhaps because it was rumored that Bond was one of the operators of the still on Piney Woods Creek.[8] The next witnesses included a juvenile female relative of Lawrence Dunnam's, several male Bond relatives, and Bond's wife.[9] Around mid-morning, the state's attorneys called Henry Bond to the stand where he answered questions until the noon adjournment. After lunch, he was then recalled to the witness box for part of the afternoon.

Final witnesses for this Tuesday afternoon included Kelly and Kelly's wife. Defense counsel hoped their answers to questioning would contradict statements made by Adams and absolve Kelly. By the time the examinations concluded, it was too late in the day to call the final two witnesses. Their testimony would have to wait until the next morning.[10]

The third day of Mancy Kelly's trial opened with the questioning of the final two witnesses. After their testimony concluded on this Wednesday, Judge Fatheree called a short recess to allow counsel to prepare their closing arguments to the court. The trial was called back into session mid-morning. E. W. Breland was the first to present his closing argument to the jury. Next was attorney E. C. Fishel, also representing the state of Mississippi. District Attorney Martin Miller gave the final summation of the state's closing argument against Kelly. Father and son duo, E. A. "Zan" Alexander, and son, Cephus Anderson, gave a valiant effort on the part of their client during their final remarks to the jury.[11] The state of Mississippi concluded its case against Mancy Kelly around 5:30 P.M. Now the jury would have to make the final decision as to the outcome of justice.

Nearly six hours later, despite the late hour—about 11 o'clock—the jury foreman read the verdict to a packed courtroom of spectators,

7/31/19 21

We the Jury find the defendant guilty as Charged.

Handwritten jury verdict from Kelly trial case 967

Convicted murderer
Mancy Kelly

MANCY F. KELLY

witnesses for both the prosecution and the defense, and family and friends of the officers and the moonshiners. The panel's decision read "guilty as charged, with no recommendations."[12] A victory for the State of Mississippi.

Mancy Kelly heard Judge Fatheree's dreaded pronouncement as he imposed the death sentence on the moonshiner about three o'clock the afternoon of Thursday, May 26.[13] The judge set Friday, July 8, 1921, as the date for the man's execution. Kelly's attorneys, Reilly, and Busby, though disappointed, immediately appealed their client's conviction. Following their filing, documents were drawn up, and court manuscripts were gathered and sent to Jackson in preparation for the appeals case to be heard before the Mississippi Supreme Court.[14]

Kelly was then transported to Jackson, where he would languish nine months in the Hinds County Jail throughout the lengthy appeals process. The state's highest court finally rendered its decision on the moonshiner's fate on Monday, February 13, 1922. The justices affirmed the decision of the Greene County Circuit Court. Kelly's death sentence would stand, and a new date was set for his execution—Friday, March 24, 1922.

In a final, desperate attempt to save the life of their client, Kelly's attorneys appealed to the office of Governor Lee Russell, in the hopes that he would grant the moonshiner a reprieve. Jubilation rose in the hearts of both counsel and client with the news of the governor's decision made public on Monday, March 13, to suspend the death sentence for Kelly. Russell explained it was because he desired "to have the State Board of Pardons pass on Kelley's application for a commutation to life imprisonment."[15]

Almost a month would pass until Kelly learned his fate. On Monday, April 10, a published list of sentence recommendations made by the State Pardon Board did not contain Kelly's case.[16] Only one of the board members, Reverend J.D. Ellis, due to religious beliefs, voted for the commutation of the sentence.[17] Kelly's legal team was then told that there would be a three-day waiting period in which the Board could yet grant a pardon. If clemency was not granted, then the death sentence would be carried out on the end of this same week—Friday, April 14, 1922.

Due to a lengthy appeals process, it was now over a year since the murders took place. On Thursday, April 13, when it became evident that no mercy would be shown by the pardon board, Sheriff Webb Walley and Deputy J. N. Sowell from Greene County arrived at the Hinds County Jail to take Kelly south to Leakesville for his scheduled execution.[18] They arrived sometime Thursday evening. Mancy was finally back in Greene County to face the gallows. He kept telling everyone he was innocent of the murder of Lawrence Dunnam but was guilty of assisting in the whiskey production. He never budged from that story. Mancy informed everyone that the rope was too big and he would not be hanged. That same night, when his sister went to say her goodbyes, Mancy reiterated to her that the rope was too big and that he refused to have it put around his neck. She said her goodbyes and left with a broken heart, still feeling her brother was innocent of the murder charges.

The next morning, Sheriff Walley asked Kelly if there was anything he requested before he was taken to the cell, where he would be held until his execution, scheduled for shortly after the noon hour. Kelly asked to see "the death trap"[19] and the rope that would be used for his execution. He commented that the rope looked bigger than he thought it should be. He was then asked if he wished to speak to a preacher. At first, Kelly said he did not want any of those but later, after Sheriff Walley insisted, Kelly requested the Baptist preacher. When it was determined that Brother Golden was out of town, Kelly finally consented to speak to Brother Hardy from the Presbyterian church.[20]

When the noon hour came, all preparations were completed for the execution to take place. Mrs. Kelly and their children were allowed to visit with Mancy one last time, in his cell, to say their final goodbyes. The visit was to be not over ten minutes long. Sheriff Walley and Reverend Hardy waited on the back steps of the courthouse, as Sheriff Walley planned to take the minister to pray with Kelly after his time with his family.[21]

Suddenly, Deputy Sheriff Nat Sowell emerged from the jail and whispered a message to Sheriff Walley. It sounded like he said, "He has cut the rope!"[22]

In reality, what Sowell told the sheriff was, "He has cut his throat!"[23]

The sheriff rushed up the stairs to the jail. Barely alive upon the sheriff's arrival, Kelly gave up one last gasp and "expired very quickly after the terrible wound" he brought on himself.[24]

Walley would later learn exactly what happened in that cold, lonely cell from Deputy Sheriff Jonathan Turner to whom Kelly spoke before dying. Turner recounted that he arrived at the cell door to escort Mrs. Kelly and the children from the jail.[25]

"The little boy said: 'Good by [Good-bye] Daddy.'"[26]

"'Be good son,' said Kelley, who kissed his wife about that time good by."[27]

Turner said he heard Mrs. Kelly say, "'Don't do that Mance.'"[28]

"Turning," said Turner, "I saw the blood gush from the neck. His hand passed over his neck first on one side and then on the other."[29] The deputy sheriff said due to dim lighting in the cell and the amount of blood from the wound that he did not actually see the knife.

What a tragic event for Kelly's family to witness! A terrible nightmare coming to an unspeakable end.

Turner then said to Kelly, "'Mancy what did you do that for?'"[30]

Kelly's reply, 'I just couldn't stand it; the rope looked to[o] big; Mr. Walley won't get to hang me, Jonathan.'"[31]

By this time, Kelly had laid down on the bed in the cell. When asked by Turner where the weapon was, the prisoner "pointed under the bed where the knife was found."[32]

Immediately, Walley sent the deputy to fetch a Dr. Faulk and a Dr. Knight, who were already waiting nearby to take care of the body after the hanging. He also sent for the preacher and Walter Kelly, Mancy's brother.[33]

Next, the sheriff went downstairs and out the side door of the jail and announced to the waiting crowd, what had transpired moments before, "The man who was to have been executed today has just cut his throat with a knife and died within two minutes."[34]

Sheriff Walley then called for the jurors to be present for the coroner's inquest. Once that had taken place, the jury verdict was pronounced, "The deceased came to his death at his own hands with a knife."[35]

The knife used was a single-bladed pocket knife that had been sharpened as fine as a razor blade. His wife shared that she was aware of his plan to commit suicide with a knife he received from an inmate in Hinds County, who had showed Kelly how to conceal the weapon in his shoe.[36]

News report of Mancy Kelly's suicide

Greene County jail where Mancy Kelly took his life

Two letters were left by Kelly. One was written Thursday night at 6:30 P.M. to fellow prisoners in the Hinds County Jail that thanked them for the consideration shown him while incarcerated there and also stated, "I had two chances to have done what I am doing: one on the way coming here but wanted to see my sweet wife and dear children and thought it would be unjust to them. Don't think anybody is responsible for this suicide but me; I do not think I ought to hang for this crime. The rope looks too big for me."[37]

The other letter was to Governor Russell and was later published in the *Wayne County News* and in *The Richton Dispatch*.[38] Both letters confirmed Kelly's proclamation that he was forever innocent of any murders of Green and Dunnam.

Letter written to Governor Lee Russell by Mancy Kelly

Thursday night, 8:30 o'clock

Hon. Lee M. Russell, Governor, and who it concerns:

I have written you two letters to please consider my case and commute it to a life-one, and no reply did I receive from you.

I feel that you should have come to the Hinds County jail and talk to me about my case but you did not come.

If you would not do anything for me yourself, you should let the men alone who are on the Board of Pardon. I'm sure they would have recommended me a sentence. Governor, you might as well to of taken your dear old mother of wife's life as to have taken mine away from me. I thought when I cast my vote for you, you was a much different man then what you are.

You haven't punished me for this at all, you have punished my sweet wife and babies, not me. For this is only a place of sin and sorrow. I feel that you and the district attorney who prosecuted me and John Adams have and will have my blood stains upon your hands. I have given my future life, and what my sweet wife and I have worked for, also the help of my old gray haired father and brothers and sister, all they could do or say seemed to do me no good.

It is a shame to the good state of Mississippi and to the county of Greene for Mancy F. Kelly to hang for the crime which was committed in Piney Woods Creek swamp on April 1, 1921. I wish the people could have seen it before it was too late. If I only could have had a chance I could have proved it to the good people that I was not a murderer. It was not my desire to ever murder a man or woman.

I hope not this case alone, but all cases, should be long remembered to the good people of Mississippi. I know that I had a man who had practiced law for seventeen years, that was a fair and law abiding citizen and lawyer of Mississippi. This is my last words: Hon. Marion W. Reilly is a fair and honest Man.

I know he believes in every man having his justice. Good people, one and all, it was not evidence that convicted me to hang alone. I wish I could talk face to face with each and every one of the county and state—face to face.

I could tell them more than they thought I knew, I have been punished for the crime I did. I hope that Mrs. Green and Mrs. Dunnam will not think that I was the cause of either of their husband's death.

> *Written and signed by*
> *Mancy F. Kelly*

Around 3:45 P.M., on April 14, 1922, Mancy Kelly's body left Leakesville in a casket for the family's burial ground just over the Wayne County Line.[39]

As the murders of Jake Green and Lawrence Dunnam had made national headlines, so, too, did the suicide of Mancy Kelly. As he had promised, Mancy Kelly never allowed the gallows rope to touch him.

It was just too big!

CHAPTER ELEVEN

Cheating the Gallows

THE velocity of the freight train barreling down the wheels of justice increased dramatically after Mancy Kelly's guilty verdict. Once Judge Fatheree's sentence for hanging sealed Kelly's fate, the Greene County Circuit Court proceeded to try the second case in the Piney Woods Creek murders, that of alleged murdering moonshiner Henry Bond. As the ringleader of the gang of moonshiners, Bond shot Green and killed him. The still that my granddaddy and Marshal Dunnam raided on that fateful morning of April 1, 1921, was known to all as Bond's Still.

The Bond family was well-known in southeast Mississippi, ". . . a family with a remarkable criminal record."[1] Henry and his wife, Ellen, had five children—Calam, Ernest, Lizzie, Virgel, and Azzie.[2] Months before the murders of Green and Dunnam, during the November session of the county Circuit Court, Henry's second son Ernest was indicted: Case 961, State vs. Ernest Bond, on the charge of "being drunk on a public road."[3] In the fall of 1920, Ernest was almost twenty and had already kept up the family tradition but had problems holding his liquor. He was now engaged in his first serious encounter with the law, a charge of unlawfully being drunk in a public place, around Richton and State Line public roads, in the presence of two or more people. Ernest Bond was doomed to follow in his family's footsteps as he had been around moonshine, its production, and distribution by all Bond family members.

Ernest and John Adams would disrupt church services at Zion's Rest Missionary Baptist Church in Sand Hill four months later.[4] (This is the same John Adams, now indicted for the Still Raid Murders of Green and Dunnam.) Ironically, twenty-two days before his death, Lawrence Dunnam, acting in his capacity as Deputy Sheriff of Greene County, would arrest Ernest Bond and Adams for disturbance during the church worship service on March 10, 1921. The date set for their court appearance was Saturday, April 9—Case 966, State vs. Ernest Bond and John Adams, on the charge of "disturbing public worship."[5]

By Tuesday, May 17, the pre-trial juror selection pool for the Bond case had been depleted. His attorneys filed a motion for special *venire facias*, as "The Jury Box is exhausted."[6] The sheriff was now bound to

Exhausted box caused trial delays

call for "as many as 80 men . . ." Of those, the court accepted only seven for the jury. Twenty more potential jurors would visit the courtroom the next day.[7]

Henry Bond's trial began the morning of Thursday, May 26, 1921, again being tried in Judge Fatheree's court. The father-and-son team of Zan Anderson and Cephus Anderson represented him.[8] The defense attorneys immediately entered a motion for a *change of venue* or location for the trial, possibly due to the fact that many in the potential jury pool might have known the defendants. The judge denied the motion. The defense team made another legal maneuver as they filed "a motion for a severance in case No. '967.'"[9] As Bond was indicted along with three other defendants—Kelly, Adams, and Morris—his legal team hoped to separate his trial from the others' names and file different charges. Judge Fatheree also denied this motion. As soon as Bond's trial began, it came to light that many of the jurors were sequestered during Kelly's trial, and yet others stood outside the courthouse while the Kelly trial commenced, which was of particular concern to the defendant and his lawyers.

About nine witnesses were examined by counsel that morning—four for the State and five for the Defense. Afterward, the slow task of picking jurors from an enlarged prospective jury pool began and ran through the balance of the day. The individuals in this group had been summoned to court the day before on Wednesday and told to report the next morning when the Kelly case ran late. When the strike of Judge Fatheree's gavel closed the court session on Thursday evening, a full panel of twelve men was in the jury box for the Henry Bond murder case. The state had accepted every one of them. The defense counsel spent much of Friday morning skirmishing with the State's counsel regarding jury selection. When six were excused, the tedious work of selecting a full panel began again.[10]

Court clerk J. W. Colbert submitted the handwritten note on Friday, May 27, the day the jury was seated.[11]

The Court instructs the jury that if you find the defendant guilty then your verdict may be in either of the following forms—

"We the jury find the defendant guilty as charged" in which event it will be the duty of the court to sentence the defendant to hang by the neck until dead—

– or –

"We the jury find the defendant guilty as charged and recommend that he be given a life sentence" in which event it will be the duty of the court to sentence the defendant to the penitentiary for the term of his natural life.

– or –

"We the jury find the defendant guilty as charged, but cannot agree on the punishment" in which event it will be the duty of the court to sentence the defendant to the penitentiary for the term of his natural life.

On Saturday, May 28, Bond's attorneys entered a *motion to quash* or excuse the entire panel of jurors.[12] Various rationales for releasing panel members included that Bond's counsel was denied the right to disqualify the jury, that many in the prospective pool were relatives of the deceased, that one of the jurors heard the guilty charge pronounced against Kelly, and that counsel believed it was an impossibility of seating a fair jury under such conditions. Judge Fatheree overruled the motion. It was time to begin the trial of Henry Bond for the murder of Jake F. Green stated in Case 967. Bond would get to tell his side of the story with the jury finally selected and in place.

When Bond took the stand to testify on Monday, May 30, it quickly became evident that he and Kelly had very similar statements as to what came about before, during, and after the officers confronted the bootleggers at the still on April 1, 1921. The only difference was that Bond claimed Green never announced himself as an officer of the law, so Bond said he shot Green in self-defense, though he never denied shooting Green in the face with his shotgun.[13]

On May 31, 1921, Henry Bond's jury returned with a unanimous verdict. The statement from the jury foreman was short and to the point,

"We the Jury find the defendant guilty as charged."[14] On Wednesday, June 1, the moonshiner was convicted and sentenced to the gallows for the first-degree murders of Jake Green and Lawrence Dunnam. Bond's attorneys immediately filed a motion to appeal.

Once the trial was over, Bond, like Mancy Kelly, was immediately transported to the Hinds County jail in Jackson, Mississippi, until the state's highest court could hear his appeal. Bond would remain there until space was available on the docket in an upcoming session of the Mississippi Supreme Court for his attorneys to try to convince the justices seated on that noble bench to overturn his conviction or commute it to a sentence of life imprisonment.

Due to the great length of time consumed by both the Kelly and Bond trials, Morris and Adams would have to wait until the next session of court for their cases to be heard. They would remain in jail until the session began in November of 1921.[15]

Unfortunately for Bond, the Mississippi Supreme Court upheld his conviction and death sentence. The justices released their decision to the press on Monday, May 8, 1922.[16] Two on the bench—Ethridge and Anderson—dissented because they did not believe Bond received "a fair trial" because the murder trial occurred in Leakesville, where Green lived, and that most of the jury pool either knew or were related to the murder victims. Their objections, however, were overruled by "the majority of the court."[17] Friday, June 16, was the date set for Bond's execution which would take place in Leakesville, Jake Green's hometown. The state's representative before the Supreme Court was assistant attorney general H. Cassidy Holden.[18]

Bond and his family constantly tried to get the governor to change his sentence from death by hanging to life in prison. A few years earlier, one of Henry Bond's brothers had received a change of sentencing from hanging to life in prison, and Henry was hoping for the same. The head jailer, Deputy Sheriff Russ Harris, after befriending Henry while held in the Hinds County Jail, even tried to get Bond's sentence commuted by using his connection with Governor Harris's father who served the Governor as his chief of security at one time.[19]

On June 14, 1922, Governor Russell granted Bond a reprieve that would allow the Board of Pardons to act upon the request to have Bond's sentence changed from hanging to life in prison.[20] The members would consider the proposal at their monthly meeting in July. Once again, Bond's hopes were dashed as the commute-to-life request failed. Bond's date of execution on the gallows was set for Friday, July 21, 1922.[21]

During Henry Bond's lengthy stay in the Hinds County jail, his family visited him several times. During one family visit in those hot, humid months of the summer of 1922, the subject of having a family member visit Bond and sneak a pistol into the jail, allowing him to use it to escape, was debated. One of Bond's sisters, Lizzie, said Henry was her favorite brother, and she would do it. However, once home, she could not find her gun, so another sister, Hattie, gave her 32-caliber pistol to Lizzie to take to Henry.

Before the next scheduled visit, Lizzie prepared lunch for Henry and brought him a small basket of tomatoes. She placed the pistol in the bottom of the basket and carefully covered it with a tomato camouflage. Lizzie then took the train from Sumrall to Jackson, bringing a possible means of her brother's escape with her.[22]

When she arrived at the Hinds County Jail, Bond's sister was allowed to visit shortly in an interview room with her brother. The siblings were allowed to talk with the assistant jailer in the room for just a few minutes. Lizzie asked the official if she could stay and eat lunch with her brother, but the jail denied her request. However, she was allowed to leave Bond the special bag lunch she had brought him from home. During the visit, Lizzie set the lunch and the basket of tomatoes on the windowsill. While they were talking, Lizzie gave her brother a special look toward the basket in the window, letting him know how "special" those tomatoes were and not to forget about them. After Lizzie left and Bond returned to his cell, he discovered the pistol concealed in the basket under the plump tomatoes his sister had brought. He kept the weapon hidden for the next few days while plotting his getaway.[23]

The day was drawing near for Henry Bond to be returned to Greene County for his hanging. He hatched a plan to escape, using the pistol Lizzie had supplied him with. On Tuesday, July 18, 1922, three days before Bond's scheduled execution date, family members were in Jackson and brought lunch to him in hopes of visiting with him. Henry's brother,

Isaac Bond, and Isaac's wife had come to Jackson to visit the governor for a last plea for Henry's life. Isaac dropped off his mother, Henry's daughter, Azzie, and sisters Lizzie and Hattie to visit that morning. Not allowed a visit during lunch, the family members delivered the lunch they brought and waited outside the jail in hopes of seeing Henry later.[24] At some point that morning, "Bond's wife and two relatives" were allowed to visit him in his cell.[25]

Soon after the visit was over and the family members had exited the jail, Russ Harris, the jailor, and trustee Henry Thomas climbed the stairwell to the third floor of the Hinds County jail to deliver the lunch to Bond that his family left for him.[26] When Harris unlocked the cell doors to hand over the sack lunch to Bond, the prisoner pulled the pistol from a concealed hiding place on his person. What ensued next amounted to a duel for freedom. Bond "placed the pistol against Harris' breast, fired and turned to run."[27] Harris fell to the floor, and Bond stepped over him to make his break. However, when he reached the door leading to the main hallway from this area of the third floor, Bond found the door locked. He immediately turned and walked back to where Harris lay on the cell block floor to retrieve keys from the jailer.[28]

When Bond started towards Harris, the deputy, though terribly wounded, raised himself a bit, pulled his revolver, and shot Bond three times, one of which killed him instantly. Bond lay lifeless in his cell.[29] Despite being hit several times, Harris could stagger to his feet after picking up the pistol used by Bond. Using his keys, he locked the cell door, shut the door to the entrance, and stumbled down several flights of stairs. Making his way to the adjacent building, Harris burst into the office of Sheriff Lewis Williams and slumped into a chair, covered in blood that continued to pour from his chest wounds.[30]

"Old Bond shot me and I am done for. I have locked up the jail and here are the keys," Harris blurted out.[31]

Five minutes later, he then leaned forward and took his last breath.[32]

Moments later, Greene County Sheriff Webb Walley, upon arriving at the Courthouse for what he thought was a mission to pick Bond up to return him to Leakesville for his hanging, was dumbfounded to learn of the prisoner's death and that of jailer Harris.

Russell Harris, Hinds County jailer

Covington County Sheriff Graham captured Bond's relatives later that night as they escaped by car, speeding toward their home in Covington County.[33] It would later come to light that the party of five relatives, once exiting from the Hinds County jail, had gotten in their car—parked a short distance from the jail—to pick up Bond once he escaped. When several shots rang out from the jail, Henry did not appear as time passed, and the five family members fled town.[34]

Henry Bond's sisters, Eliza "Lizzie" Bond Lott, and Hattie Bond Slade would be transported back to Jackson and remain in the Hinds County jail for four months until indicted for "aiding Bond in his attempted escape and also carrying deadly weapons into the jail."[35] Neither woman was indicted for murder.[36] The Bond sisters would plead guilty to the charges levied against them. Eliza received a two-year sentence in the Mississippi State Penitentiary at Parchman, located in the Mississippi Delta; Hattie would serve a six-month sentence at the same facility.[37]

Bond was now the second convicted felon to cheat the gallows of the four indicted for the murders of Jake Green and Lawrence Dunnam. He also became the fifth man to die in connection to the dreaded April 1, 1921, Piney Woods Murders.

Useless deaths over dreaded moonshine.

Henry Bond and Jackson Jailer Killed in Pistol Duel

Jackson, Miss., July 18.—Almost within the shadow of the gallows where he was soon to pay the extreme penalty for the murder of a prohibition officer in Greene County, Henry Bond shot and killed Rush Harris, a Hinds County jailer, here today and the condemned man was killed in return by Harris who, although mortally wounded grasped his gun and fired.

The double killing is the culmination of a series of tragedies that have surrounded the case and it is the second time the gallows has been cheated of its victim in connection with the same case.

Maney Kelly, who was jointly convicted for the murder of the officers was also condemned to death. He was confined to the Hinds County jail until the day before the one set for his execution. Everything was set for the execution and just as the sheriff reached his cell he drew a knife and slashed his own throat, dying a few minutes later.

Bond was tried shortly after, and he too, was sentenced to die. The Supreme Court affirmed the decision, but Governor Russell granted a reprieve until July 21 in order that the board of pardons might review his case. It did and refused to commute the sentence. Since that time Bond has been a model prisoner, seemingly reconciled to his fate.

This morning relatives of Bond arrived in the city and asked permission to see the condemned man. Jailer Harris granted the request.

Shortly after they left, Harris went to Bond's cell on a tour of inspection. While investigating conditions, Bond suddenly drew a revolver and fired twice, both bullets taking effect in the breast. Drawing his revolver Harris killed Bond instantly. Picking up the latter's gun he walked to the Court House, climbed a high pair of steps and made his way into the sheriff's office, where he laid down both guns and incoherently related the story. He expired a few minutes after.

The shooting for which the pair were condemned to die occurred on April 1, 1921, when Bond, Kelly and John Adams were surprised at a still in the wilds of the swamps in the corner of Greene, Perry and Wayne counties. The officers commanded them to surrender but instead they opened fire and Jake Green, prohibition officer, and W. L. Dunnam, town marshal of Richton, in Perry County were killed.

Adams, the third member of the gang turned state's evidence and got off with a life sentence.

Relatives Arrested

Jackson, Miss., July 19—Charges of conspiracy to murder were lodged today against the wife, brother and two other relatives of Henry Bond, condemned murderer, who assassinated Russell Harris, Hinds county jailer, Tuesday afternoon, and was shot to death by the jailer while vainly trying to escape from the third floor of the jail.

The relatives of Bond were captured last night by Sheriff Graham of Covington county, while they were speeding southward in an automobile towards the family home in Greene county.

Evidence has been secured, according to the authorities showing that the family of the murderer not only smuggled into the county jail the pistol with which Harris was assassinated, but that they had participated in the plot to murder, and were in waiting in an automobile near the jail to take Bond out of Jackson in event his dash for liberty should prove successful.

DR. R. M. COCHRAN

It is with pleasure we present the formal announcement of Dr. R. M. Cochran, as a candiate for Mayor of the Town of Richton, subject to the action of the Democratic primaries to be held next month.

Dr. Cochran has been a citzen of Perry County practically all of his life, and for the past several years has practiced his chosen profession in the town of Richton, being too well known to every citizen for us to attempt any elaborate introduction.

His announcement is the result of a strong personal solicitation from a large portion of the best citizens of the town, as it was their opinion that he would make an official second to none.

Dr. Cochran's friends do not believe he will have any opposition for this important office, but predict, even if he does, that he will win in a walk. We commend his candidacy to the careful consideration of every voter.

News report of the deaths of Bond and Harris

CHAPTER TWELVE

Cohorts in Crime

THE trial for Will Morris, the third of the men indicted in the Still Raid Murders, was postponed due to the delay concerning jury selection and the fact that the trials took longer than expected. A *special venire* or panel of prospective jurors, instructed to appear at the Greene County courthouse the morning of Friday, May 27, 1921, were told once they arrived that "they could go and unless notified later to come back."[1] Morris was freed on a $1,000 appearance bond[2] and told to appear in Greene County Circuit Court on Monday, November 14, 1921, to face the charges outlined in Case 969—manufacturing and distribution of intoxicating liquor.[3]

Six months later, Will Morris finally had his day in court. Once again, Judge Fatheree would preside, as he had for the trials of the other defendants in the Piney Woods Creek murders. Once again, Zan and Cephus Anderson would be representing this defendant in Judge Fatheree's courtroom. Defense counsel immediately filed a motion for a change of venue.[4] The motion was denied. Next, the court moved on to the charges filed in Case 969 and heard Morris's testimony regarding his activity in participation in the making and distribution of intoxicating liquor.

At the time of the murders, Morris was a farmer[5], around age thirty-five[6], who lived near the still. He and Bond ran the moonshine operation together.[7] As a close friend to Bond, Morris had returned with his injured friend to Bond's home and was present when Dr. Cochran made his house call. By the time the good doctor arrived, Morris was quite intoxicated and "made the first confession which involved the other three men."[8] Due to Morris' testimony before the court that he did not have a weapon at the still on the day of the murders, the murder charges (Cases 967 and 968) were dropped.

Throughout the days of the trial, the State and the Defense both presented their evidence. Once they each presented their closing arguments, the Defense filed numerous jury instructions. The last of these read as follows:

"The Court further instructs the Jury for the Defendant that unless they believe from all the evidence beyond all reasonable doubts and to a moral certainty that the Defendant operated or assisted in the operation of a whiskey still as charged in the indictment it would be the sworn duty of the Jury to promptly acquit the Defendant."

Filed November 24, 1921
J. W. Colbert[9]

The jury in this certain Greene County Circuit Court courtroom found Morris guilty. Before sentencing, the Anderson legal team filed a motion with the court requesting a new trial.[10] As with others previously filed, the motion was quickly denied. With no other impediments or arguments before the bench, the judge sentenced Morris to three years of hard labor at the Parchman Farm (later to be called the Mississippi State Penitentiary) in Sunflower County. Following the trial's conclusion, Morris was transported some two-hundred-seventy-three miles northwest of Leakesville to serve his time in the state's central prison.

While Morris was incarcerated at Parchman, several of his friends wrote a Petition of Pardon and submitted it to Governor Russell for his consideration to shorten Morris's sentence. The petition stated, "that the Mother of Will Morris is very old and feeble and that she is Blind, and that she grieves very much and longs for his presence."[11] To my knowledge, the governor did not grant this petition, and Morris served his entire sentence before leaving the state prison.

❖ ❖ ❖

S.S. "Sid" Baggett was a farmer from Sumrall, Mississippi, the fourth moonshiner punished for his part in the Piney Woods Creek murders. According to newspaper accounts, it would not be until Tuesday, April 5, that authorities arrested Baggett for his part in the murders.[12] The next day, he was taken to the Hinds County jail in Jackson, as had Adams, Kelly, Bond, and Morris.[13] Two federal Prohibition agents, Ellis S. Chapman and Glenn O. Whitehead, oversaw the transfer.[14] Both officers had been in Leakesville, having arrived early the morning after the murders.[15]

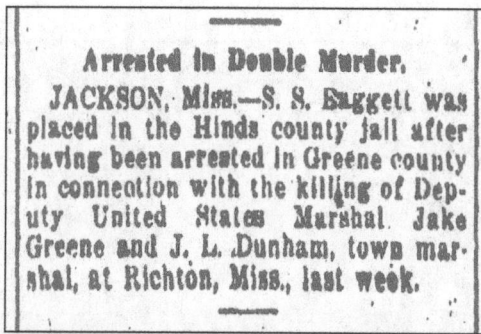

> **Arrested In Double Murder,**
>
> JACKSON, Miss.—S. S. Baggett was placed In the Hinds county jail after having been arrested In Greene county In connection with the killing of Deputy United States Marshal. Jake Greene and J. L. Dunham, town marshal, at Richton, Miss., last week.

Headline from *Evening Star* newspaper in Washinton, D.C., about Sid Baggett's arrest

One irony of how newspapers reported breaking news in the 1920s is that reporters had very little turnaround time to confirm or cross-check information. As such, news stories contained misspellings of many personal names. Baggett's was one of these. The article "Double Tragedy Marks Still Raid," which ran in the *Greene County Herald*, listed Baggett's first two initials as "B. B."[16] That same news story stated that Baggett was the one "who drew the diagram which guided the unfortunate officers to the spot of their doom . . ."[17]

Although we'll never know, it appears that Baggett may have been playing both sides against the middle. Another newspaper article reported that "he was claimed by authorities to be the man who gave the alleged moonshiners advance notice of the coming of the revenue officers to the still where the two officers were killed."[18] Many people I spoke with while investigating the murders suggested that Baggett may have been trying to eliminate competition, as he was a moonshiner.

Though I've searched diligently for any trace of news about Baggett's trial and sentencing, I have little to show for it. One last news account did mention that Will Morris was there at Parchman Farm, for a short window of time, with Sid Baggett, who was serving his sentence for his part in the murders.

Though the details are vague, I take comfort that justice was served for these two cohorts in crime.

Will Morris' appearance bond

INDICTMENT

THE STATE OF MISSISSIPPI,
Greene   COUNTY } ss.

In the Circuit Court of   Greene   County, at the   May   Term,

in the Year of Our Lord Nineteen Hundred and   Twenty-one

The Grand Jury for the State of Mississippi, taken from the body of good and lawful men

of   Greene   County, in the State of Mississippi, elected, impaneled, sworn and charged to inquire in and for said County, in the State aforesaid, in the name and by the authority of the State of Mississippi, upon their oaths present:

That   Will Morris, Mancey F. Kelley, Henry A. Bond and
John Adams

in said County, on the   9th.   day of   May   , A. D. 192 1 ,
did unlawfully and feloniously make, manufacture and distill,
spirituous, vinous, malted, fermented and intoxicating liquor

contrary to the form of the Statute in such case made and provided, and against the peace and dignity of the State of Mississippi.

District Attorney.

Indictment against Morris and others

CHAPTER THIRTEEN

Saving His Hide

JOHNNY Adams's path to facing his legal consequences would look markedly different than that traveled by either Kelly or Bond. Called as a witness during Mancy Kelly's trial in May of 1921, Adams had confessed under oath on the witness stand for his part in the killings.[1] It would not be until the Greene County Circuit Court session in November 1921[2] that Adams would join his partners in crime—Kelly, Bond, and Morris—and be brought before the court to face the charges of Case 969, involving the manufacture and sale of moonshine whiskey, for which all four men were indicted. Adams pled guilty.[3]

Adams sat in jail until Saturday, May 27, 1922, when his trial for charges levied against him in Cases 967—the murder of Jake Green— and 968—the murder of Lawrence Dunnam—opened.[4] Time was of the essence as this was also the last day of the Greene County Circuit Court's May term. Defense counsel filed a motion for a *continuance*, asking the court to postpone the trial until later.[5] Perhaps the main reason for this action, according to the continuance motion, was that Adams had "been unable to hire Counsel to defend him."[6] As such, the court appointed Zan and Cephus Anderson, who had also represented Henry Bond at trial, to represent Adams. However, that selection did not occur until "the day before the case was set for trial," Friday, May 26.[7] The continuance motion to delay the trial "until the next regular term of this Court" was denied.[8]

State of Mississippi
vs
Johnie Adams.   No. 967&968.

   Now comes Johnie Adams a citizen of said State of Mississip
pi who was indicted for the killing of Jake Green and Lawrence
Dunham on April 1st, 1921 and by motion asks the Court to
continue the above case until the next regular term of this
Court for the following reasons towit;

   1st. The Defendant has been unable to hire Counsel to
defend him in the trial of his case and the Court has appointed
Cephus and E.A. Anderson to defend the Defendant, said
appointment having been made the day before the case was set
for trial and the Defendant has not had time to counsel
with his attorneys and has not had time to properly prepare
his defense with them.

   2nd. That there is a witness Will Morris who is now
in the State penitentiary who was near the scene of the
tragedy and the said Will Morris were here he would swear
that as he was running from near the scene after the pistol
shots had been fired he observed this Defendant and that
the Defendant was not at the place or near the Deceased
when the Four shots were fired into the back of Lawrence
Dunham but instead was off some distance. This witness would
exhonorate that said Defendant from firing these four shots
into the back of Lawrence Dunham, Defendant cannot prove this
fact by any other witness that the said Will Morris and that
this witness is material in the defence of the Defendant.
The said Will Morris is within the jurisdiction of this Court
and that the Defendant can easily have him here at the next
regular term of this Court.

   3rd. Defendant has another witness , Frank McKinzie,
the Jailor at Hattiesburg, Miss., and if the said witness was
here would swear that the Defendant Johnie Adams was promised
or led to believe that if he would tell the truth for the state
in the trial of Mancy Kelly and Henry Bond for the killing of
Jake Green and Lawrence Dunham that that the State would not
hang him or try to take his life, but would show him leeniency
in the trial of this case. The Defendant does not know of any
other witness at this time that he could prove this fact by, and
that he can have this witness here in Court by the next regular
Term of this Court if give time to get them here.

   State of Mississippi
   County of Green.
   Personally appeared before me the undersigned authority
in and for said County and State, Johnie Adams, who after
being first duly sworn on oath testifies that to the best of
belief and knowledge that the attached motion is correct as
therein stated for the continuance of this case to the next

Adams requests a continuance of Cases 967 and 968

The trial regarding the "State of Mississippi vs Johnie Adams"[9] con-
vened during the Circuit Court's morning session.[10] (Often, my research
found Adams's first name spelled different ways in various documents—
Johnie, Johnny, and Johnnie—with Johnnie being the most common).

One year earlier, in the May 1921 trials of Mancy Kelly and Henry Bond, Adams had provided testimony that helped to convict the pair. Adams was "the only eye witness" besides Kelly and Bond to the Piney Woods Creek murders.[11] Almost immediately after being arrested in early April of 1921, Adams agreed to turn state's evidence in hopes of receiving a life sentence instead of being hanged.[12]

The State called several witnesses, including Greene County Sheriff Webb Walley, who was present when Adams first confessed to his part in the murders at the still on April 1, 1921.[13] Walley detailed how Adams confessed to having fired three shots at Officer Green and missed but with the intent to kill him. He also confessed to his part in the plot to kill the raiding officers.[14] The Defense declined to call any witnesses.[15]

Case 967: State vs John Adams

Closing arguments for Case 967 ended "at 10:38 a.m."[16] As he had before in the trials of Kelly and Bond, Judge J. D. Fatheree gave specific jury instructions concerning the panel's deliberations.[17]

"The Court instructs the jury for the state that if you believe from the evidence in the case beyond a reasonable doubt that the defendant either by himself or in aiding, encouraging and assisting Bonds and Kelly, or both, killed J. F. Green without authority of law and with the deliberate intention of taking his life you shall find Adams guilty."

Filed May 27, 1922
J. W. Colbert, clerk

Counsel for both the State and the defense each filed jury instructions. Those for the State were refused; instructions for the Defense were accepted.

Jury instructions from the Defense for Case 967:[18]

"The Court further instructs the jury for the defendant that if they believe from hearing all of the evidence in this case that the defendant did give evidence in behalf of the State in the trial of the case of Mancy F. Kelly and Henry Bond in securing their conviction, then the jury would be warranted in putting theirselves [themselves] in the place of the defendant and look from the standpoint that the defendant was placed in as a witness in behalf of the State in concluding a righteous verdict, and may take into consideration these facts in giving any recommendation the jury desires of leniency to the Court on behalf of the defendant."

Filed May 27, 1922
J. W. Colbert, clerk

Soon after, the jury began their deliberations. The courtroom crowd hoped that Adams would get the same sentence as Kelly and Bond, the death penalty. Even though his version of the events of the April Fool's Day murders conflicted with Bond's and Kelly's recollection, Adams convinced the state's attorneys to go with his rendition of the facts. Adams testified that he participated in the shootings, but had turned and run from the site. When he did, he became entangled in some briars. He claimed Kelly shot Dunnam in the back while Adams was away from the area. However, Bond and Kelly testified that Adams was still there. Deliberation did not take long at all regarding the charge levied in Case 967, as a decision was announced "at 12:05 o'clock."[19] Adams was acquitted for the murder of Jake Green, "We the Jury find the defendant not guilty as charged in the indictment."[20]

After the court took a lunch break, the portion of the trial reserved for Case 968, the murder of Lawrence Dunnam, began. By entering "a technical plea of guilty," Adams took responsibility for his part in Dunnam's death.[21] In hopes of seeking leniency with the court, Adams entered a plea of manslaughter instead of murder; however, the district attorney did not accept the petition.[22]

Because a plea was entered, Judge Fatheree was then free to impose a sentence, consequently, for this second murder without having to send the case to the jury. The judge sentenced Johnny Adams to a life of incarceration on a second count of murder for Lawrence Dunnam's death. Adams was never prosecuted for his violation of the liquor laws, as punishment for the possible conviction of that lesser charge was now a moot point.[23]

As the sun set on this chapter in the saga of the Piney Woods Creek murders, Johnny Adams was transported to Sunflower County, Mississippi, where he spent the remainder of his life incarcerated at Parchman Farm. While there, Adams was killed in a confrontation with a fellow inmate in 1939.

PART III

The Green Widow's Draglines

"If you want to understand today you have to search yesterday."

—Pearl S. Buck

CHAPTER FOURTEEN

No Friend Dearer than Jake

ARTIN V. B. Miller first met Jake Green in December of 1912 when the latter was elected Sheriff of Greene County. Both were on the same side of justice as Miller was a criminal prosecutor in nearby Meridian. From the start, the men developed a strong, supportive friendship based on mutual respect and genuine affection for each other. Sometime before 1920, Miller became the District Attorney for Mississippi's 10th Judicial District. This Circuit Court district, which had been established by the Mississippi Code of 1906, was comprised of "the counties of Lauderdale, Clark, Wayne and Green."[1]

Miller's recommendation of Green came in a series of letters to Mississippi Congressman Pat Harrison. This portion of a letter written by Miller to Harrison on December 12, 1919, on Jake's behalf sheds light on how much the district attorney thought of my Granddaddy Green,

"Pat, I am very anxious to do something to help Jake land with this fellow Gantt [head Prohibition agent in the Atlanta office] if he wants the job. No man has been a closer friend to you than Jake Greene, and he is still your friend. Some people in Greene County have their knife out for you good and strong. But they have never been able to shake Jake or say of his kindred or friends. He is a friend to both of us, and his kind of friendship counts for something."[2]

Though Harrison had already selected a man and seemed determined to remain true to his decision, Miller's well-penned notes written during the application process evidently were able to persuade him otherwise. Also, when Green received the appointment, Harrison wrote Jake a letter on February 6, 1920, and encouraged him to make sure Jake appropriately thanked Miller for pushing him through to gain the position.[3]

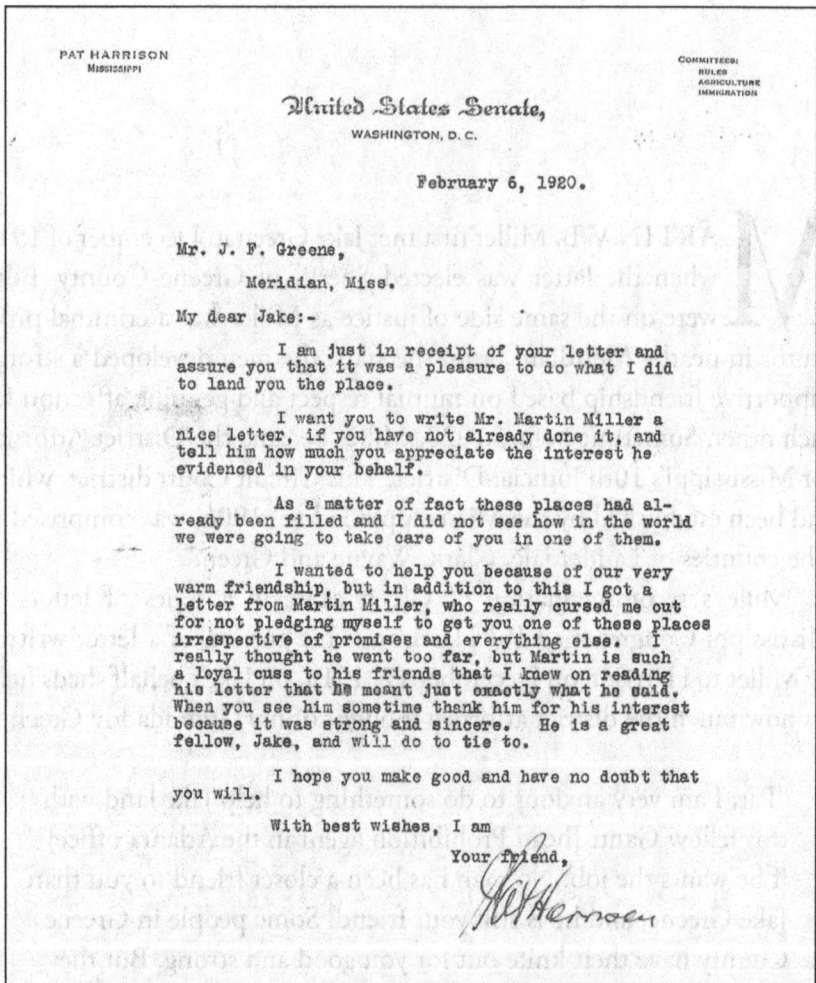

PAT HARRISON
MISSISSIPPI

COMMITTEES:
RULES
AGRICULTURE
IMMIGRATION

United States Senate,
WASHINGTON, D. C.

February 6, 1920.

Mr. J. F. Greene,

Meridian, Miss.

My dear Jake:-

    I am just in receipt of your letter and assure you that it was a pleasure to do what I did to land you the place.

    I want you to write Mr. Martin Miller a nice letter, if you have not already done it, and tell him how much you appreciate the interest he evidenced in your behalf.

    As a matter of fact these places had already been filled and I did not see how in the world we were going to take care of you in one of them.

    I wanted to help you because of our very warm friendship, but in addition to this I got a letter from Martin Miller, who really cursed me out for not pledging myself to get you one of these places irrespective of promises and everything else. I really thought he went too far, but Martin is such a loyal cuss to his friends that I knew on reading his letter that he meant just exactly what he said. When you see him sometime thank him for his interest because it was strong and sincere. He is a great fellow, Jake, and will do to tie to.

    I hope you make good and have no doubt that you will.

    With best wishes, I am

        Your friend,

Letter from U.S. Senator Pat Harrison congratulating Jake on his appointment as a Prohibition Special Agent

From the moment he received the devastating news of Jake's death, Martin Miller positioned himself squarely in the middle of all aspects from investigating to prosecuting and beyond. He worked tirelessly to gather the right evidence to be used against the moonshiners, even if it meant allowing Adams to receive a lighter sentence than others' full convictions and maximum sentencing. He would serve as the lead prosecutor in the trials for all the men indicted for the Still Raid murders. Once the trial dates were set, Miller was committed to using every legal influence possible to secure guilty outcomes for all individuals involved. This mission became a part of Miller's being and remained for him a driving force to stay connected to the family Jake left behind.

Miller promised Eliza and the children that he would assist in any way that he could. This promise went on for decades. He continued to send letters of concern for the grieving family, which often included financial assistance. For many years, Martin Miller sent letters at Christmas. From the wording and tone of his letters written to Eliza, Miller conveys an underlying tone of bearing an obligation to assist Jake's survivors. The district attorney's letter, written to Eliza the first Christmas she and the children went through without Jake, is especially moving.[4]

Miller's letters were part of Mimi's stash of memorabilia my sister Lisa preserved in the Spider's Sack (my term for paperwork related to the murders that my grandmother stashed away in a brown paper sack). From heartfelt words expressed in these surviving letters Miller penned, he seemed to feel a great responsibility for Jake's death, as his had been such a pivotal role in my grandfather's appointment. This portion of a letter Miller wrote to Eliza on December 21, 1932, is especially poignant,

> "Christmas time is a time when naturally your mind runs
> backwards and not forward - - you think of those you have met
> in life's journey that you really care for most, and when I am in
> that mood I always think of Jake."[5]

When death comes so unexpectantly, it's those small gestures of support that help fill the void left by lack of financial support. These gestures of kindness did not stop. For many years afterward, Miller continued

M. V. B. MILLER
ATTORNEY AT LAW
MERIDIAN, MISS.

DISTRICT ATTORNEY
TENTH DISTRICT OF MISSISSIPPI

December 23rd 1921.

Mrs. J. F. Green,
McLain, Miss.,
Dear Mrs. Green:-

For some reason, I feel like Christmas to me,
cannot be complete. It seems to me that I ought to be getting
some little rememberance to send to Jake. I can't help but
feel that he is with us, and feeling that way, I can appreciate
in a very very small degree, your feelings. I want you to know
that I know and understand.

I never expect to have a dearer friend, a friend
who loves me more than he did. As we quickly journey Life's
highway, it is not our fortune to meet and know many whom, when
the acid test is applied, that we can call friend.

Let me say this, a slight word of consolation to
you, that while our hearts bleed it is far from his wish that it
should be so. It is his wish that we should put from our hearts
the great sorrow and let his memory serve to warm and gladden our
hearts; if he could speak to us now, this would be his message.

Give my love to all the children.

I wish for all of you, a gladsome Christmas and a
Happy New Year.

I am,

Your friend,

MM:LS.   Martin Miller

Attorney Martin Miller's letter to Jake's survivors at Christmas 1921

to send letters and financial aid for the support of Green's family. These
letters were kept in Mimi's collection of memories that could have been
lost in the ashes of her burn barrel. How glad I am that they ended up in
her spider's sack.

Martin stayed a true friend to Jake's family.

CHAPTER FIFTEEN

"Gethsemane"

J AKE and Eliza were faithful members of the Leakesville United Methodist Church. Many good memories were made within its walls when he was around. Eliza and her children kept their place in the church family after Jake's death. By the 1950s, a sizeable sum of money had accrued from donations made in memory of Jake to the Leakesville United Methodist Church (LUMC). For years, Eliza had contemplated how to spend the memorial money. Twenty-eight years after Granddaddy Green's death, Eliza decided to use the funds to commission the creation of a new stained-glass window and donated it to the church. She wanted something that would leave a lasting legacy on the church and the community. Entitled "Gethsemane," the multi-colored panes show Jesus praying in the garden of Gethsemane with his disciples the night before His crucifixion.

While investigating several stained-glass window companies, she determined that J.M. Kase, Inc. Stained Glass Studios, out of Reading, Pennsylvania, would get the honors. The company, which opened its doors in 1888[1], was a "nationally famous glass studio."[2] After many letters were exchanged with the company during the planning process, she carefully ordered, on October 6, 1949, a unique stained-glass window to be placed behind the pulpit and above the choir loft at LUMC. Eliza sent specific instructions to the glass company about how she wanted the window to look and the proper placement of such a treasure. She agreed to send a check for $200 as a deposit and the balance of $155 upon shipment of the finished product. The J. M. Kase Stained Glass Studios began creating the memorial window.

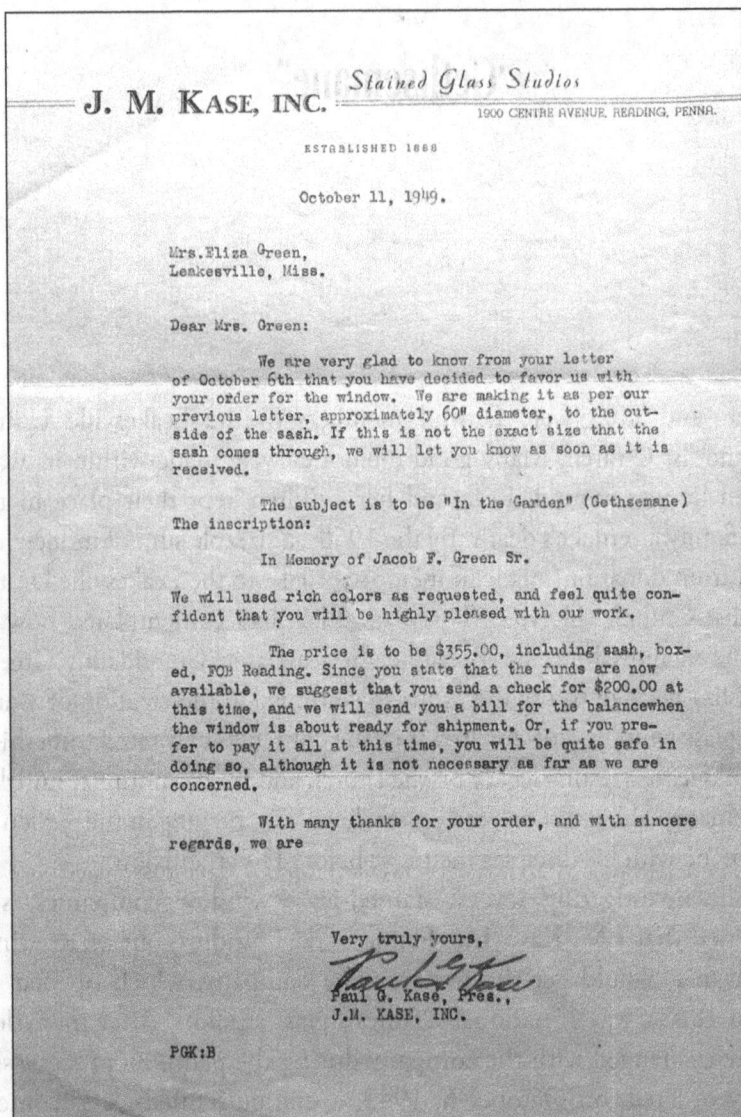

J. M. KASE, INC. *Stained Glass Studios*

1900 CENTRE AVENUE, READING, PENNA.

ESTABLISHED 1888

October 11, 1949.

Mrs. Eliza Green,
Leakesville, Miss.

Dear Mrs. Green:

We are very glad to know from your letter of October 6th that you have decided to favor us with your order for the window. We are making it as per our previous letter, approximately 60" diameter, to the outside of the sash. If this is not the exact size that the sash comes through, we will let you know as soon as it is received.

The subject is to be "In the Garden" (Gethsemane) The inscription:

In Memory of Jacob F. Green Sr.

We will used rich colors as requested, and feel quite confident that you will be highly pleased with our work.

The price is to be $355.00, including sash, boxed, FOB Reading. Since you state that the funds are now available, we suggest that you send a check for $200.00 at this time, and we will send you a bill for the balance when the window is about ready for shipment. Or, if you prefer to pay it all at this time, you will be quite safe in doing so, although it is not necessary as far as we are concerned.

With many thanks for your order, and with sincere regards, we are

Very truly yours,

Paul G. Kase, Pres.,
J.M. KASE, INC.

PGK:B

Letter from the company that manufactured Jake's memorial window

When the special order finally arrived at the church, the shipping crate contained several, separate pieces, with metal bars all around. Eliza was a strong-willed individual. Upon opening the box, she found assorted and seemingly mismatched pieces of multi-colored glass and lead stripping within. My grandmother did not like what she saw, and so, on March 17, 1950, Eliza complained to the glass company in a letter. Paul G. Kase, president of the company, responded on March 20, 1950, and assured Eliza that she would be delighted once the window was installed.[3] True to the man's statement, the design was breathtaking once the window was in place. "In Memory of Jacob F. Green" graced the bottom curve of the circular window and would be the only wording found on the window piece.

For once, Eliza was speechless and may have even shed a tear or two, as before her was the most exquisite piece of stained-glass art she had ever seen! It became a showpiece for all who attended or visited the Leakesville United Methodist Church. The church later added lighting in the sanctuary to enhance the window's appearance at night, making it look magical.

"Gethsemane" window at Leakesville United Methodist Church

My daddy, Polly, would stand tall in front of that window for his entire lifetime attending Leakesville United Methodist Church, sometimes as the music leader or when business meetings were conducted. Polly and Ruth's children were married in that church, and Jake's stained-glass window was frequently featured in many pictures. We all stood and faced it as we declared the Apostles Creed each Sunday morning. The prayer in front of the window became a tradition of respect for both Granddaddy Green and my God.

The Apostles' Creed[4]

I believe in God, the Father Almighty,
maker of heaven and earth;
And in Jesus Christ His only son, our Lord;
who was conceived by the Holy Spirit,
born of the Virgin Mary,
suffered under Pontius Pilate,
was crucified, dead, and buried;
the third day he rose from the dead;
he ascended into heaven,
and sitteth at the right hand of God the Father Almighty;
from thence he shall come to judge the quick and the dead.
I believe in the Holy Spirit,
the holy catholic church,
the communion of saints,
the forgiveness of sins;
the resurrection of the body,
and the life everlasting.
Amen.

Momma would always make sure to turn the left porch light switch on for the night services at the church, so we could enjoy the brilliance of the stained glass—a tradition I carried on after she was gone. When I have visited the home church on various occasions, I have faced that window with the utmost respect for my Savior and the artistic representation of our Lord's last hours on earth. Often, while singing the old hymn, "Lead me to Calvary," I pondered the window's meaning: to never forget Gethsemane, the ultimate sacrifice. Jake gave his ultimate sacrifice while killed in the line of duty. I would always glance at the wording "In Memory of Jacob F. Green" as I left the sanctuary. All I knew was that the window of colored glass was one of the only physical remembrances I had of my Granddaddy Green.

Andy and Juanita on their fortieth anniversary in front of Jake's window

The Leakesville United Methodist Church has used a picture of the stained-glass window to adorn the cover of the weekly bulletin they used for Sunday services for years. It's just another blessing to see Jake's memorial window on those documents, but more as the centerpiece for services at the church.

That piece of art will always have a special connection to the past but gives us a glimpse of our eternity beyond the window through its brilliant colors.

CHAPTER SIXTEEN

My Daddy's Last Year

MIMI died on July 24, 1987, at the age of ninety-six. Lisa's daughter Elizabeth was born on Daddy's birthday, November 12, 1987. Though he had told no one, Daddy had been sick, not sharing his health secret with anyone until after Elizabeth's birth. He then decided to go to the doctor; the results were not what we wanted to hear. The dreadful "C" word was now a part of our family vocabulary. He had cancer of the stomach. His treatment involved an innovative procedure for receiving cancer treatments at home. That was in November of 1987.

Daddy scheduled a special Polly Wiggle Joy Corporation meeting for December 17, the week before Christmas. (My father, uncle, and cousin formed this organization to manage the Camp Polly Wiggle property owned by Granddaddy Green's heirs.) Two main topics were on the agenda: Wiggle's death and Daddy's medical issues, as they pertained to the corporation. Throughout the past sixteen years, tragedy and loss inserted themselves into our family's life again. Daddy's sister Bernell died in a tragic car accident on June 26, 1971. Seven years later, the family's organization was incorporated on November 15, 1978, with Polly, Wiggle, and Bernell's daughter, Joy, as mutual stockholders of three hundred shares. Four years after, in 1982, Joy sold her shares to Polly and Wiggle, and they now owned 50% of the corporation each. Daddy was President and Treasurer, and Wiggle was Secretary.

A year before Daddy's cancer diagnosis, his brother Wiggle died on October 30, 1986, in a car wreck caused by a brain aneurysm he suffered while driving. His shares were equally divided between his sons, Billy and Jim. Daddy explained I would be appointed as a director and receive a new assignment as interim treasurer in the event of his incapacity. At that meeting, my dad gifted fifteen shares to each of his children—Jake, Debbie, Lisa, and me. The remaining ninety shares would transfer to Momma upon his death.

We all went to Momma and Daddy's for Christmas that year for one big family reunion. Daddy adorned himself in his traditional red Christmas jumpsuit that Momma had made. He was in the best spirits, and everyone soaked up the festivities. We were not sure if it would be the last with Daddy. Precious memories!

Paw Paw Polly with my son, Andrew Jacob, sitting in front of pictures of the three Jacob Francis Greens

In May of 1988, Daddy asked if he could talk with me privately. He then pulled out the brown leather satchel in which he kept all his Polly Wiggle Joy Corporation paperwork. After my daddy unbuckled the front closures on the pouch, he took out the following: business checkbook, incorporation paperwork, tax papers, copies of the stock certificates, the corporation seal, and various miscellaneous documents. He said he had some old papers in the back that were just family stuff. Then, Daddy told me something that would let me know he knew he would not get any better. He wanted me to take over as treasurer of the Polly Wiggle Joy Corporation. My heart sank as I thought of this unwanted position of responsibility. However, my daddy had entrusted me with it, and out of respect, I would never let him know my true feelings.

After handing over the satchel into my care, I remember that Daddy continued to get weaker and weaker. At that time, I felt he knew what the future held for him, and his days were dwindling. I felt honored that he had asked me to fill his shoes and do this because he took great pride in the satchel's contents. I took the bag home and placed it in the back of my closet, not knowing what I had in my hands then. It would be years before I discovered what was behind the corporation checkbook in the backside of the case.

In June, Daddy ended up in Forrest General Hospital in Hattiesburg. Mom stayed with him daily, but we all took turns sitting with him at night. On July 1, 1988, it was my turn to stay with Daddy. Momma was there, and when it got bedtime, she went and stayed at Uncle Brac and Aunt Virginia's, which was only a few blocks from the hospital. It was just Daddy and me. We talked some, but he was tired and uncomfortable, and it got to the point in the middle of the night when he needed some extra pain medicine. It seemed like an eternity to get the nurses to deliver his relief, but it finally came, and he dozed off.

When breakfast arrived on schedule, I cut the pancakes up and fed them to Daddy. He spoke a few words and ate only a little. Momma came, and soon after, the doctor arrived. He checked out Daddy's chart and listened to his chest. He then told Momma it wouldn't be long, and they just wanted to make him as comfortable as possible. It could be days or hours, but his suffering would be brief. They would give him some medicine to help him rest. Momma and I called the immediate family members and told them they needed to get to the hospital as soon as possible.

The nurse brought in a thick foam mattress that they would put on his bed to make him more comfortable. She asked Momma and me to step out while they were putting him on it. Momma and I walked down to the end of the hall where the nurse's station was and the elevator. Neither of us said much as we waited.

I remember the nurse rounding the corner and telling Momma and me we needed to hurry to the room. When we got there, they told us he

Daddy and Consuelo Moreno at the Leakesville 4th of July Parade 1976 (photo courtesy of *Greene County Herald,* July 1976)

was going fast. With Momma on one side and me on the other, we held Daddy's hands as he took his last breath. Although I was trying to be strong for Momma, I was breaking up inside. I stepped outside the room to call the rest of the family members to let them know not to come to the hospital but to meet us back at the homeplace in Leakesville. Daddy's earthly struggle had ended, but ours had just begun. Mine still lingers.

Daddy died on a Saturday at 11:35 A.M., right before noon. We sat with him until Freeman's Funeral Home from Leakesville arrived to pick up his body. Momma and I drove home and met up with the rest of the family. We did not want to affect the community's Fourth of July events, so we decided to have his Celebration Service the day before on July 3rd. He, like his father Jake, was buried the next day after his death.

For years, Daddy played the part of Uncle Sam in the annual Independence Day parade in Leakesville. He grew a beard most years to make his character look authentic and looked forward to the event and the part he played. Different family members, since his passing, have played his part as Uncle Sam in the annual parades. The Fourth of July was very special to Daddy; he shared his love of country with us. That holiday, however, would never be the same.

My daddy's traditions were important to him, so they are our traditions: God, Family, and Country.

CHAPTER SEVENTEEN

My Homeplace

IN October of 1991, Andy and I decided to take Momma up on her offer to buy her house in town. She first talked to us about purchasing the home after Daddy died in 1988, but we declined. With Andy working so much at night, having another adult in the house would ease his conscience when he was out working. The only stipulation we gave her was that she would live there with us. We would be raising our kids in my homeplace.

I contacted the office of our local newspaper, the *Greene County Herald*, about placing an advertisement for the sale of our present house, which was in the Pine Level Community just outside of Leakesville. Cheri Turner Culpepper, whose family owned the newspaper, worked in the paper's ad department and had been tasked with producing our ad. She called me and asked if I would consider delaying the advertisement by a week to allow her and her husband to come to look at our house. Dennis and Cheri Culpepper bought the house and wanted to get in by Christmas. The sale of our home allowed us to accept Momma's offer to buy her house. Andy and I worked feverishly and packed all our belongings in two months. That was the end of the story on the Pine Level house.

As there was not enough room for our household items and my mother's many collections, she decided to distribute her family heirlooms among her children. I can remember sitting around the table in the dining room putting four piles on the table and drawing numbers to decide what order to pick cherished items. Jake's wife, Carol, knew a lot about antiques and the value of older pieces, so we let her put the piles together. As Momma watched us draw from her chair, my brother, sisters, and I sat around the table and laughed and cried. Although we swapped a few keepsakes, each of us received precious momentos from Polly and Ruth's lifetime of living in that home. Several things that Momma had acquired belonged to Jake and Eliza. During the last years of her life, Momma had the opportunity to visit each child's home and see "her stuff" displayed.

Rufus and Hazel Walley

❖ ❖ ❖

The old house needed gobs of work to modernize and adapt to fit our family's needs. The cabinet doors in one of the downstairs bathrooms were sorely in need of repair. I received a recommendation to use a man named Rufus Walley, who lived right over the Greene-Perry County line on the outskirts of Richton. After making an appointment to meet with him, we drove to his home. He was waiting for us in his shop, located beside his house. We gave him all the instructions and measurements required for refinishing our cabinet doors during our visit. He said he would inform us when he completed the job.

As we turned to leave Mr. Rufus' workshop, he asked me to whom I belonged. I told him I was from Leakesville and was Polly and Ruth Green's youngest daughter.

Then, Mr. Rufus stated, "Well, Little Lady, I need to apologize to you. My uncle killed your grandfather."

I was so dumbfounded and shocked at his statement. I could not believe he was apologizing for something he had no control over that happened so long ago. I stood speechless as he shared that his uncle had been Mancy Kelly, one of the men indicted for Granddaddy Green's murder, who committed suicide before being hanged.

Still in shock, I talked with Mr. Rufus about what he knew about the incident. He shared a few stories passed down to him from his father about Mancy and the case. He said he would like to take me to the property, located not far from his home, where the crimes occurred. Mr. Rufus said he could arrange for us to visit the property, and we made plans to come back and meet with him.

Andy and I drove back home in disbelief at what had just occurred. Mr. Rufus had no clue as to the effect his apology would have on my future. We continued remodeling the house, and I put the "Mr. Rufus Visit" on the back burner.

Procrastination gets you nowhere, but I know God's timing is everything.

❖ ❖ ❖

I resigned from my teaching position to stay home to help with Momma's needs during the last three years of her life. On the weekends, my siblings would take turns coming to the homeplace and attending to her on the weekends, which gave me a break. My bunch would then stay at our camp that Andy had recently completed building.

Daddy would have been so excited to know we had a home in Son Kittrell's "Polly Field" adjacent to Camp Polly Wiggle! My dad and Mr. Kittrell shared many hunting and fishing adventures on and around the Chickasawhay River swamp. The Green and Kittrell families held a close relationship during my lifetime and still do to this day. To acquire some of Mr. Son's property to build a camp on, which was on the river and sharing borders with the Green family property, was only a God-thing. He did it again. We could drive to our camp and enter a field where Daddy and I used to hunt, and now I had a house situated smack dab in the middle of that old cow pasture.

Andy and I lived in the homeplace with Momma until she died in 2002. Afterward, we remodeled her bedroom and purchased the first set of new bedroom furniture in our time as husband and wife, as we had been using hand-me-downs from other family members.

It had always been our dream to move to our camp near the Chickasawhay River once we retired from our jobs with the state. Andy and I had talked about this on numerous occasions. He had been kind enough to move to the homeplace for me to help with Momma, so now it was my turn to make a concession. One night, over dinner, I caught my husband totally off guard when I told him that I would actually be happy to sell Momma's house and move to our camp if he would make some additions to the structure. Amazed, he asked me what it would take to live there, and I wrote a list for him. Andy started the project the very next day. He didn't want to give me a chance to change my mind about moving to the woods.

During the summer of 2005, rumors were circulating throughout Leakesville that we might consider selling our house. Dorian Dickerson Heindl called me and asked me not to put the house on the market since she and her husband, Fred, were very interested in buying it. They wanted to purchase a home in Leakesville as a second home and keep their primary residence in Brandon, Mississippi. Dorian was one of my mother's home economics students at Leakesville High School and a classmate of my brother Jacob, who also went by the nickname Jake.

She became an extension home economist, an advisor employed by the government to assist people in rural areas with methods of farming and home economics. Momma was also one, and she and Dorian would judge each other's county fairs each year. Dorian adored Momma.

As my parents' homeplace was very close to the home where Dorian grew up, it would allow her to help her mother when needed. A few months later, in August, we sold my parents' home to the Heindls. Dorian was tickled to be getting Mrs. Ruth's house. However, she and her husband did have to wait a short time to move in due to our agreement to turn over the house only when our addition to the camp house was complete.

Juanita's parents' home on Alabama Street that she and Andy renovated

Unexpectedly, I received an offer in April of 2006 to become principal at Leakesville Elementary. After much prayer, consideration, and my husband's blessing, I accepted the position. Andy continued building the camp addition, and he and our son Drew moved in as soon as the building was livable. Due to my new job, my daughter Paige and I stayed in town at the homeplace until July and joined our guys during the summer break.

The change of residency for us has been a positive move. Yet, I still make monthly drives by the homeplace to reminisce, and when I do, I always glance across the street to Mimi's house. The Smith family still owns the house, but nobody has ever taken care of the house and yard as Mimi did. I can still hear her say, "Go back and trim around that pecan tree a little closer, girl. And make sure you shut the gate when you get finished."

Mimi's house will always be her and Jake's homeplace, and right across the street is mine. No more people with Jake Green connections live on Alabama Street.

The Green Widow with all her spiderlings in the 1940s

Polly Green with his little family 1960s

Daddy and Uncle Wiggle celebrating Mother's Day with Mimi

Polly (left), Wiggle (right), and Mimi at her 95th birthday celebration

CHAPTER EIGHTEEN

The Satchel

WHEN I resigned from my fourth-grade teaching position at Leakesville Elementary School in 1999 to stay home with Momma due to her declining health, I found out that I had time on my hands I had never had before. During those first few months of being at home, I decided to investigate the leather case of paperwork that Daddy gave me before his death that contained the Polly Wiggle Joy documents and some additional papers.

On one of my last school field trips with my students, we visited the Old Capital Museum in Jackson. While there, I noticed a document on one of the walls that reminded me of one of the papers I had glanced at in Daddy's satchel. Until then, I had only used the corporation checkbook it held to pay bills. In the back section of the bag was a set of papers that Daddy told me little about. Seeing this museum exhibit reminded me that now was the time to investigate the contents of the leather case further.

I could hardly wait to get home from the field trip. Once there, I immediately retrieved the satchel. After removing the documents from the front section, I picked each one up and pondered why Daddy would keep it. Deeds, wills, letters, legal documents, and other transactions must have been important to Daddy, but he never mentioned them to me.

Next, I dove into the pouch's back section and began looking for the document I thought looked like the one I saw at the Old Capital

Museum. Finally, I found it! One of the yellowed parchment documents, folded so carefully, was an 1825 Land Grant to Clayton Smith signed by J.Q. Adams. For a few minutes, I could hardly breathe as the significance of this moment began to sink in—a document signed in 1825 by the President of the United States. Though in awe of what I held in my hand, I could not figure out why my father would have this document. I had to investigate the validity of the signature to confirm that it was what it appeared to be. My teacher's eye compared each letter's strokes and confirmed that this was probably indeed a document signed by John Quincy Adams. I was holding a precious piece of American History that became part of my family history.

Amazing! Thanks, Daddy.

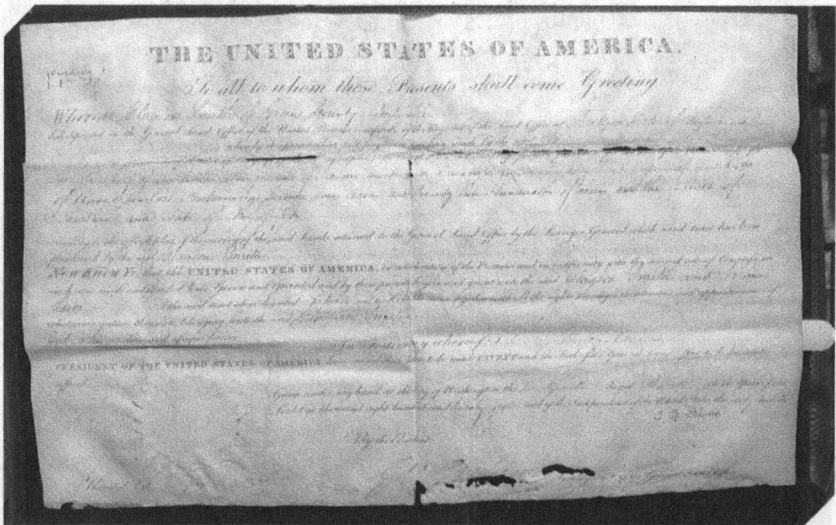

1825 Land Grant deed signed by U.S. President John Quincy Adams

I examined the last will of Doctor Bodo Otto Adams, my great-great uncle, who purchased the Polly Wiggle camp property before the Civil War and during the Yellow Fever Epidemic. During the epidemic, he was practicing medicine in Mobile, Alabama, and chose to move north to escape what he thought was the cause of the fever: the heavy fog of Mobile Bay. Bodo had his niece and nephew, Jacob and Elizabeth McClean, and their children, come from New Orleans to live on his property and assist in caring for him until his death. Due to his need for personal assistance at and around his property, he already had two ladies who worked for him: Moriah and Margarette Smith. After his death, Adams left most of the property to Jacob and Elizabeth McClean. However, in his will, he designated a small parcel of land, some livestock, and use of his homestead without payment for one year after his death to his two "faith women"— Moriah and Margarette—for their dedicated service to him.

There were deeds in the satchel dating from the 1800s and 1900s. Some were in a court folder envelope on which Daddy wrote in pen, PROPERTY OF JACOB F. GREEN. Though I had recognized my father's writing on the folder, I had somehow overlooked the lighter

Treasures found in Daddy's satchel

handwriting in the background. Years later, while on my journey of discovery to better understand my grandfather's story, I rechecked the satchel's contents and noticed that the darker writing on that folder didn't match the lighter. The words, *Private Papers of J.F. Green, Sheriff, Leakesville Miss*, were handwritten in ink. The faded words were not my Daddy's handwriting at all. They were Granddaddy Green's!

The folder's contents now made more sense as the mystery unfolded. That specially labeled folder contained all the property deeds given to Granddaddy Green when he purchased the properties from the Jacob F. McClean Estate beneficiaries. That's why Bodo's will was in there, too. It was all the paperwork from when the McClean's Uncle Bodo had purchased the property, from the early 1800s until the Civil War. I then laid all the documents in chronological order before me, and they all lined up from beginning to end. I now knew where the Camp Polly Wiggle property originated and how it got purchased and passed down through generations for me to hold in my hands.

In the back of the old leather satchel that Daddy had entrusted to me was a historical gold mine! So many answers to long-posed questions were revealed within the leather case—a family history. It took me years to understand each one's role. Piece by piece, each document revealed its particular significance to me. The satchel became part of my family's history story, and its contents answered questions that, up until now, had only been hearsay.

We all have one of those "satchels" hidden somewhere within the cobwebs of our family's history. Yours might be in a box, in an old suitcase, tucked away under the eave in an attic, or sitting beside you at your supper table. Please don't wait on them to reveal themselves. Go looking or asking before it's too late. We might not be proud of all its contents or even want to share it with others, but by fate or by choice, it is our history.

Preserve it for your family and yourself.

CHAPTER NINETEEN

The Spider's Sack

AS I assisted Momma with her many health challenges, we became closer than best friends. It was a blessing to ensure she had the best care at home. Although she enjoyed visiting with family and friends in person, she also used the phone to check on loved ones.

Bernell's daughter, Joy, and Momma always stayed in touch. Joy decided to come for a visit, hoping it wouldn't be the last with Ruth. My first cousin and I began discussing family history during her time with us. I shared the satchel's contents with her to see if she knew anything about the documents found within. As Joy and I were sitting in the dining room, looking through the contents of the leather case, my sister, Lisa, arrived at the house.

After listening to Joy and me talk about the contents, she casually mentioned that she had a paper sack of paperwork that she had hidden from Daddy when they were cleaning out the middle room at Mimi's. Lisa said the bag was in her safety deposit box at the bank. I was unaware any such documents existed, so I asked her if she would go to the bank and get them for us. Lisa left immediately.

Once back from her trip to the bank, Lisa showed us the items she had retrieved—a small paper lunch sack and a few more oversized items. She placed her treasures on the table for us to look at. Reaching first for the paper sack, she started pulling things out. I was in awe of its contents. How could so much family history be in such a small sack? Within that humble, brown paper bag, I found answer after answer to questions I had pondered for so long concerning the before, during, and after of Granddaddy Green's death.

Taking a deeper look at the contents, I saw:

- Letters before his appointment as Federal Prohibition Agent
- Letters after he took the position of prohibition officer
- Letters and postcards that Jake had written and sent to Eliza from wherever he was working
- Documents, telegrams, and newspaper clippings about the day he was murdered
- Letters of condolences from all over the state and country
- An envelope with negatives and pictures printed of his gravesite on the day of his funeral
- Cards from the floral arrangements with pins and green ribbons still attached

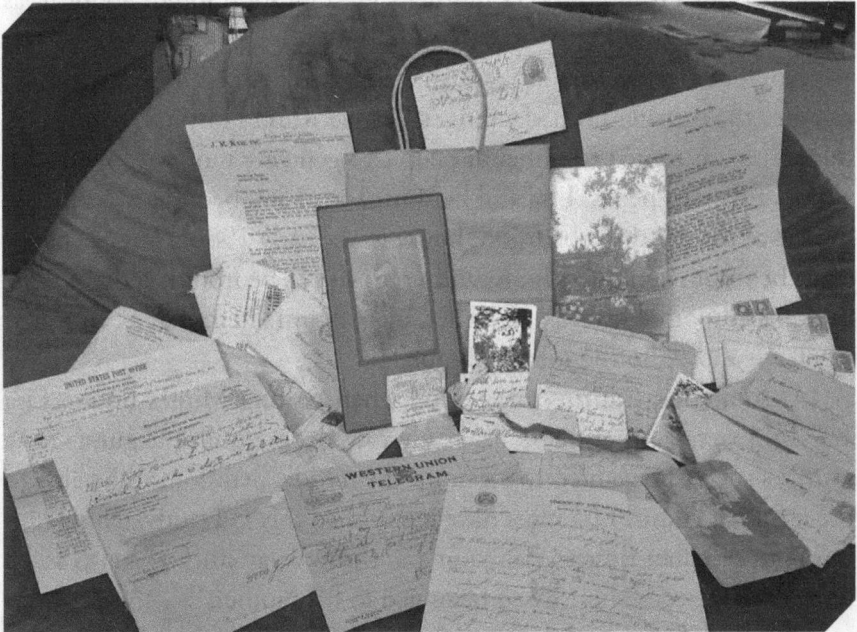

The trove of documents and photos found in the Spider's Sack

As the three of us continued to sit around the table and sift through the relics before us, Lisa shared how she had gained possession of these treasured documents. She reminded us that when our grandmother broke her arm in 1978, Lisa had moved in briefly to help around the house. As you will remember, Mimi was not always the warmest person to be around. Although I had always kept the family code and never asked Mimi or Daddy about Granddaddy Green's death, my sister Lisa—being Lisa—asked our paternal grandmother all kinds of questions related to our family's history. Surprisingly, I learned that day from my sister that many deep and personal conversations about Granddaddy Green followed.

Lisa went on to say that our grandmother showed her papers she had saved from when Granddaddy Green gained the position of prohibition officer and documents concerning his death. Mimi even showed her the white gift box in which she had stored them, hidden in her bedroom, pushed far in the back of her built-in chifforobe. Though it was intriguing, at the time, to learn of this mysterious collection of archives from Granddaddy's Prohibition-era murder case, Lisa soon forgot about it, as life was busy and full.

Not long after Mimi's broken arm had healed, our grandmother chose to enter the nursing home facility at Greene Rural Hospital. Afterward, the house was rented to different people to generate money to help with Mimi's financial needs. Lisa and her husband, Tom, became two of these renters of Mimi's three-bedroom house in the early 1980s. They kept the front bedroom as a guest room and used Mimi's bedroom as theirs. The middle bedroom, however, was where all of Mimi's items had been stored when she moved to the nursing home

At some point during the period when renting Mimi's house, Lisa and Tom were getting the house ready to welcome multiple guests for a visit. As such, she wanted to clean up the middle bedroom to be able to use it for her guests. Lisa must have mentioned this to Daddy, telling him it was an excellent time to clean out and throw away stuff. She also asked him for help, as the house had belonged to his mother.

Together, father and daughter began looking through all the boxes, bags, and a closet full of Mimi's items. Daddy gathered the first items he thought were unimportant and took them outside to the burn barrel found under the old magnolia tree in the backyard. He started a fire with those first items and went back repeatedly to retrieve more items from the middle bedroom. He would gather armfuls of clothing, papers, magazines, hats, purses, whatever he could get his hands on, take them out, and toss them in the burn barrel. When Daddy had his mind set on something, we all knew better than to question him.

As Lisa and Daddy worked together that day, in what I believe was divine inspiration, she started thinking about the box of papers that she knew contained memorabilia pertaining to Granddaddy Green's death. She understood our dad would want to get rid of anything related to those memories. Watching for her window of opportunity, Lisa exercised some bravery and sprang into action. When Daddy took out his next load of items to the burn barrel, Lisa rushed into Mimi's old bedroom, opened the door to the chifforobe, reached way back into the deepest part, and secured the gift box of treasured papers. Quickly shoving the box under her bed, she rushed back to the middle room before Daddy knew what she had done. She didn't want him getting his hands on those precious papers and burning them with everything else.

My sister tried to save as much as possible that day, as she and our dad continued cleaning out the middle bedroom. From his actions, it was evident that Daddy planned to burn any old documents or papers he could find, perhaps connected to many memories of things that had little emotional meaning or perhaps brought out too many feelings for him. Soon after the burn-everything episode, Lisa took the box of memories and transferred its contents in a small paper sack for safekeeping in her safety deposit box at the Bank of Leakesville.

❖ ❖ ❖

When Mimi was still living in the house, she would write or have Lisa write the names of whoever she wanted an item to go to after her death. Pictures, pottery, dishes, trinkets, costume jewelry, and furniture were there. Some she wrote in pen, some in pencil, and some in chalk. We guessed her thinking was that if she got mad at someone, she could easily wipe off and change the name.

I have several things of Mimi's that I still treasure in my home. I received a framed print of the painting "Pinkie," and Ashley, my twin cousin and Joy's daughter, received the matching picture, "Blue Boy," the originals having been works of eighteenth-century painter Thomas Laurence. Mimi had two granddaughters, born to separate parents, on September 4, 1963. Mimi was a great-grandmother in the morning when Ashley was born in Hattiesburg. Later, the same day, she gained her sixth grandchild, as I was born in the Leakesville Hospital. That doesn't happen too often.

Creamer and sugar set marked for me by Mimi

I also have a sweater, some pottery, a painting, a vase, costume jewelry, and various scarves, hats, and hat boxes. I even ended up with some letters and pictures of Mimi that show a softer side I never got to know. One of my favorite articles of memorabilia is her wooden Wahoo Board! When I was a child, my grandmother and I had many significant competitions on that board. That's where I must have gotten my competitive nature.

All the items I received from Mimi's personal belongings are precious to me, and I've shared many of them with my children and grandchildren.

However, nothing I have compares to the contents of the Spider's Sack that Lisa snatched from its hiding place and secured its contents in her safety deposit box. How blessed I am to have been allowed to discover the Green Widow's pouch of treasures.

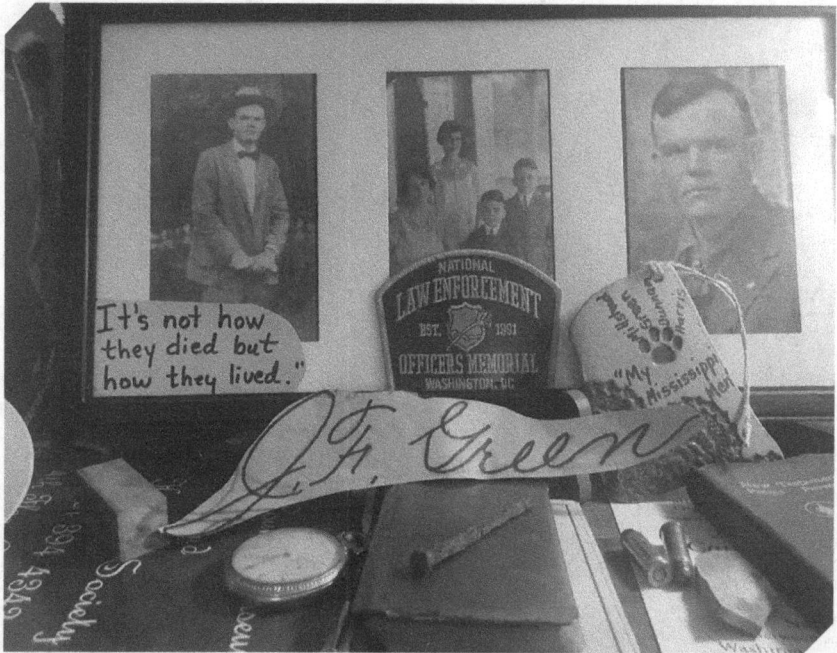

My daily inspiration

I had no idea what a simple brown paper sack would do to my future! Its discovery shook up my world in a good way. That sack would become one of many treasures unveiled as I continued my search for answers that nobody could tell me where to look.

That day, I was inspired to start a deeper, more thorough investigation into Granddaddy Green's death and was encouraged to search out any information I could accumulate on my journey.

PART IV

Clearing Away the Cobwebs

"... Sweep down the cobwebs of worn-out beliefs ..."

—ELLA WILLCOX, 1883

CHAPTER TWENTY

Walking in the Same Shoes

M Y husband, Andy, became a conservation officer for the Mississippi Department of Wildlife, Fisheries, and Parks (MDWFP) in 1991. He had gone through the application process in 1987 when Daddy was still alive. He was one of two who made it through the interviews yet fell short of his goal. Although he never saw Andy in an officer's uniform, Daddy was incredibly proud of my husband. The MDWFP hired my husband four years later, in 1991, a few years after Daddy's death. Andy finally had his dream job! He was now a Conservation Officer (Game Warden) for the State of Mississippi and was assigned to serve Greene County. Another law enforcement officer in the family.

One Tuesday, Andy told me he was going on an assistance call with the Greene County Sheriff's Department but could not tell me how long he would be gone or share any details of the assignment. I didn't think anything of it because he was always helping the sheriff with various assignments. Little did I know it, but Andy stepped right into my Granddaddy Green's footsteps. He led a joint operation of the Greene County Sheriff's Department, officers of the Alcoholic Beverage Control, and federal ATF agents into one of the most extensive whiskey-still raids in South Mississippi, in an area known as the Mt. Pisgah Community of Greene County, south of Leakesville. Knowing the wooded areas around the still, Andy had been selected as the best man for the job.

The raid took place early the next morning on Wednesday, November 18, 1992. According to an article that ran in the *Greene County Herald*, the raid was "the second-largest moonshine still . . . found in the state since 1972."[1] My husband told me afterward that he felt a little like Granddaddy Green probably felt as he was sneaking into the area and recognizing the noises of a working still. The operation was successful, as authorities arrested those involved and shut down the modern-day moonshine operation. Seized in the raid from the operation run by an Alabama man were "44 55-gallon drums of bran mash . . . , a pickup truck, 1,000 pounds of sugar, 150 pounds of wheat bran, 400 new plastic one-gallon jugs, and other miscellaneous items . . ."[2] Later that day, ATF officers used explosives to destroy the still.[3]

Andy and other officials after raiding moonshine still in November 1992 (photo courtesy of *Greene County Herald*, November 1992)

Ironically, my children's father, grandfather, great-grandfather, and great-great-grandfather were all in law enforcement. All four were a part of different raids on illegal stills, decades apart. This portion of Daddy's election campaign from 1947 speaks of his love and respect for Granddaddy Green, "My father, the late Jake Green, died in the service of our country that we might have less lawlessness about us. His

JACOB F. GREEN IS A CANDIDATE FOR SHERIFF OF COUNTY

WILL BE TAX COLLECTOR OF GREENE COUNTY, AS BOTH OFFICES GO TOGETHER

Coming before the voters of Greene county, is J. F. (Polly) Green, of Leakesville, who authorized us to announce his candidacy for sheriff and tax collector of Greene county.

Mr. Green needs no introduction from us, as he has lived here all his life except time he spent in the U. S. armed forces in camps and overseas.

high school and attended junior

He graduated from Leakesville college at Raymond, Miss., and is well qualified for the office he seeks. His statement to the voters of the county follow:

To the Citizens of Greene County:

I would like to take this opportunity to officially announce my candidacy for the office of sheriff and tax collector of Greene county.

The encouragement and solicitation of my friends have definately made me a candidate for this office.

I am a native son of Greene county, and my interests are here with you for a clean and wholesome place to live.

My father, the late Jake Green, died in the service of our country that we might have less lawlessness about us. His inspiration is my inspiration, and I hope to be able to serve you in the future as my father did in the past, as a square shooter and friend to my fellow man.

My services in World War II amounted to three and half years, of which sixteen months were spent overseas. I am proud to have been of service to our country, and hope you see fit for me to serve you in the important capacity of sheriff and tax collector of Greene county.

JACOB F (POLLY) GREEN.

WHISKEY STILLERS, CAR ROBBERS AND OTHERS ARE JAILED

Sheriff J. F. Green and the state alchohol tax men, swooped down on a 240 gallon copper still last Thursday and destroyed 24 barrels of mash, brought in the still and 1,290 pounds of sugar, 26 bags of charcoal and one croaker sack full charcoal, and three men, Herman Finch, Steve Finch and Claude Gipson are out on $1,000 bond each awaiting the grand jury.

Sheriff Green and one deputy and the alcohol tax men found the still in beat one about a mile south of highway 24, east of Big Creek and on a branch.

Six Mobile, Alabama, boys, Paul D. Cazalas, age 18; Donald Berry, age 16; Luke Brown, age 17; Thomas Hildreth, age 17; James Stringer, age 18, and Archie Jones, age 16, are held in the county jail here and are charged with grand larceny.

They were caught taking tires, etc., by night watchman John Denmark, but left in their car, and he and Sheriff Green overtook them Tuesday morning about 6 a. m., east of Leakesville.

Sheriff Green also cleared up about two weeks ago some cattle stealing in this county.

Polly Green's 1948 still raid while Greene County's Sheriff

Polly's announcement for candidacy for sheriff

137

inspiration is my inspiration, and I hope to be able to serve you in the future as my father did in the past, as a square shooter and friend to my fellow man."[4]

Though Andy never served as sheriff of our county, Jake, Daddy, and my husband are men cut from the same cloth—honest, loyal, and true.

Daddy had shared with Andy the feelings he had as sheriff, and they had several talks about Daddy's adventures raiding stills. Daddy even showed Andy a copper-looking item he said he had recovered from one of the stills he raided in 1948. Daddy kept it in his barn at the Leakesville homeplace. Years later, Andy told me that the pot in which I was growing flowers on our front porch was a part of a whiskey still that Daddy had raided. It was another piece of prohibition history, right under my nose, added to the list of paraphernalia from the past.

Andy had his own "Bootlegging Stories" to share with Daddy and me. When he was a young child, his father assisted in distributing moonshine all around south Mississippi. He shared that his dad would fill the back

Moonshine still relic holds flowers on my front porch.

of the vehicle with weighted objects so that it would not appear noticeably different when he would load the trunk up with moonshine. Andy was raised on the other side of the moonshine madness. He was growing up in the 1970s, but it was still illegal to transport and sell liquor in a dry county. He remembered riding in the back of the car, sitting atop bottles of shiny. Then twenty years later, as a state law enforcement officer, my husband would be on the right side of justice. Law enforcement officers were in the minority when it came to the moonshine business. Many individuals made their living manufacturing and distributing the liquor, while others tried to uphold the laws that prohibited its existence.

My great-grandfather, grandfather, father, and husband all played parts on the right side of the gun. Each one of them faced, at one time or another on their duty posts, individuals who did not want to abide by the laws regarding their lucrative business of moonshine.

Mimi became the only widow in our family to be born out of the madness of prohibition. Her grandmother, mother, my momma, and I could have played the same part, but we were blessed not to have to step into her shoes.

CHAPTER TWENTY-ONE

More Kelly Family Encounters

IN 2004, after staying home with Momma for three years, I returned to the classroom; Leakesville Junior High hired me as a sixth-grade teacher. Once there, a co-worker convinced me to join BeautiControl Cosmetics as a sales rep with her. I was required to attend a training meeting in Mobile, Alabama, about an hour from Leakesville. At the meeting, each of us was placed into a different group. As we went around the table in my group and introduced ourselves, one of the younger ladies introduced herself as Tiffany Walley Smith from Richton. I took a shot in the dark and asked her whether she knew a Rufus Walley.

She said, "Sure do. That's my Paw Paw!"

She assured me he was still living when I asked if he was. After I told her how I knew him and about his apology, she gave me his phone number.

When I returned home from the meeting, I called Mr. Rufus about scheduling a meeting with him and taking me to visit the Piney Woods Creek property where Granddaddy Green had been killed. I asked Mr. Rufus to wait until our family had an opportunity to meet, as I wanted my extended family members to join us. He said that would be fine. We met a few weeks later, and everyone agreed they wanted to come with me. I called Mr. Rufus and scheduled to meet with him. Before the date to meet him came around, I received devastating news. Mr. Rufus Walley had open heart surgery and died from complications. I was heartbroken that we never reconnected.

Procrastination . . . no . . . God's timing.

Fast forward to January of 2015. The Greene County Distinguished Young Woman Program had a Retreat at Camp Polly Wiggle. My sister, Debbie, and I had volunteered many times before with this organization, and Debbie asked me to tell the girls the history of Camp Polly Wiggle, including how it got its name. In preparation for the event, I sat at my computer to search for new information to add to my presentation. I keyed into the search box the name of the man responsible for Granddaddy Green's death, Henry A. Bond of Richton, Mississippi. Maybe something would surface about the murders that I could share in my presentation. Up came . . . Jacob F. Green/ATF and Cases reported, Cases Argued and Decided in the Supreme Court of MS Oct. Term 1921, and March Term 1922.

I sat in awe as I read the words on the computer screen. These links contained information about Granddaddy Green's death that was more than I had ever known or knew existed.

Later that night, at the camp event, as I shared with the young ladies my standard remarks of Camp History and how the place got the name Camp Polly Wiggle, I included the story about meeting Mr. Rufus and his apologizing to me for his uncle killing my grandfather.

In the middle of my sharing of Mr. Rufus, one of the young ladies raised her hand and yelled, "That was my Uncle Rufus!"

This young lady was Rufus Walley's great niece, Taylor Meadows.

I asked her about Hazel, Rufus' wife, and if she was still living.

Taylor said, "Sure is; she works at the Fish House," a local eatery.

Taylor gave me Mrs. Hazel Walley's contact information during a break in that evening's session. I could hardly wait to get home.

After calling Mrs. Walley and scheduling a visit, I called Debbie and asked if she wanted to go with me. Debbie and I had a wonderfully enlightening meeting with Miss Hazel. When we arrived, we met David Smith, a close family friend of Rufus's, whom Hazel had called to be with her. They shared what they knew or had heard about the Piney Woods murders. Miss Hazel told us that Rufus had researched what he could find out at the Greene County Museum.

Mr. David had his father's stories about Mancy Kelly and his part in the murders.

They both talked about Mancy Kelly's personality and what they had heard about the murders. Mr. David and Miss Hazel presented varying accounts of Mancy's participation in the April Fool's Day still raid. She said he was a good man who just got caught up with the wrong bunch of friends. I shared with them what information I had stumbled upon. The plot thickened with each story we exchanged. Mr. David also shared that, at one time, he had owned the property on which the still was located. He explained how he purchased it from one of the paper companies but had since sold it to a Nicholson Family. Mr. David offered to contact the present landowners—Kevin and Cassie Nicholson, who had inherited the land from Kevin's father—to ask about planning a future trip to the property for me. He drew me a crude map of the area that placed the site downstream from the bridge and squarely on Nicholson's land.

Near the end of that afternoon's visit, Miss Hazel told Debbie and me about Diane Goodnight, Mancy Kelly's great-niece. Diane's grandmother had been Mancy's sister. Miss Hazel believed Diane would have some family history to share with me. I was so excited!

Like every other clue, I could hardly wait to see where this new one might lead. When I called Diane, she agreed to meet me at her home to discuss details she knew might help my research. Although this introduction to Diane represented the other side of the coin, I wanted to make as many connections as possible and learn all I could about the men involved, when they died, and where they were buried.

Once at her home, Diane led me to her beautiful back porch. As we sat and visited, it was like we were friends already. She shared her family Bible that had in it the Kelly Family Tree. I took pictures of the diagram and found the Taylor Meadows connection. Diane also shared stories that her grandmother, Catherine Kelly Rich—Mancy Kelly's sister—had shared with her.

One of those stories Diane told me was the one her grandmother had told her about Uncle Mancy's death. Her grandmother said Mancy made moonshine, like many did in those days, to make extra money for financial needs. When he got arrested, ended up with a guilty verdict, and was given a death sentence of hanging, the family was devastated!

Diane gave me the last new bits of information: the burial locations of Johnny Adams and Mancy Kelly. Adams' grave was in Frisco Cemetery, and Kelly's was in Hollis Creek Cemetery in Wayne County, Mississippi.

CHAPTER TWENTY-TWO

Discovering Uncle Johnny

IN the spring of April of 2016, I searched on FindaGrave.com to see if I could find where each man involved in the murders was buried. This information would assist me in determining the death dates for each of the individuals. The website offered details for a Johnny Adams of Perry County, Mississippi, buried in Frisco Cemetery. Diane Goodnight had mentioned that Adams was possibly buried there, so I felt good about the visit. But would this Johnny Adams be the one involved in the murders? I got pictures of the grave marker, just in case, and all the other Adams markers in that cemetery.

It wasn't long after I visited Frisco Cemetery that I made an appointment to meet with the Perry County Historical Society to try and gain answers to some of the questions I had about the Perry County characters in my mirage of individuals. I called the president, Sarah Magee, and she invited me to come to the May Meeting. She posted a notice in *The Richton Dispatch* to ask anyone who might have information about the 1921 murders on Piney Woods Creek to attend the meeting. I showed my research and presented it to the group at a Baptist church, just outside of Richton. I was just trying to get the word out and hoping I might get a bit of information from those in attendance.

I introduced myself and informed them that I was seeking out any information on "either side of the gun" to put the pieces together of what happened on that April Fool's Day of 1921, with the murders of Jake

Green and Lawrence Dunnam. I shared that I had talked with Diane
Goodnight, Mancy Kelly's great-niece, and she had shared her family's
story about her great-uncle.

I also told my audience that I had visited Frisco Cemetery to take
pictures of a grave that might have belonged to one of the convicted
men, Johnny Adams.

When I said that, an older lady who had come in with a younger man
and sat to my right said to the crowd," Hey, that's my Uncle Johnny!"

I was in shock when she said that, but I did not want to get too
excited. I asked if I could talk with her after I was finished with my
presentation. She obliged, and I was thrilled!

Well, as soon as my presentation was over, I dashed over to her table.
She introduced herself to me as Janie Adams Hollingshead. She told me
that she read an article in *The Richton Dispatch* about me being a guest
at the Historical Society and was curious if we were connected by having
the same last name. (Sometimes, misspellings of my last name occur by
placing an "s" in the word—Hollingshead. Also, some family members
include the letter "s" in the name.) She said she was divorced from the
Hollingshead man, and it had not been a pretty marriage.

Then we got to discuss her connection with Johnny Adams. He was
her uncle and she was little when he died. She recalled him being in
prison and told me that that is where he had passed away in 1939 from
wounds suffered in a fight with a fellow inmate. Janie said her uncle was a
kind man to her and tried to give her a pet rabbit one Easter years before
he went to prison. She shared that her Uncle Johnny was planning on
getting out of prison and opening a bakery. That was really all she could
remember about him. Janie was, at that time, eighty-two years old.

I tried to go visit her several times to hopefully gain a picture of
Adams, but she was always busy. She did tell me to make sure I called
before I came, since she packed a shotgun for protection! A very special
encounter, to say the least, and one not expected, but so glad she ven-
tured out that day.

God continued to surprise me.

CHAPTER TWENTY-THREE

Cecelia's Contributions

I N January of 2016, Andy contemplated running for a position on the
Greene County Board of Supervisors and decided to put his name in
the hat to serve our district. He completed his application to qualify
and asked me to deliver it to the Greene County Circuit Clerk, Cecelia
Bounds. After turning in Andy's paperwork, I talked with Cecelia about
how far back her court documents went or if she had access to any records
from 1921. I explained that I wanted to research my grandfather's death
further and hoped she might lend a hand.

She said no documents that old were housed in her office, but some of
them might be found in the Greene County Historical Museum, located
on the top floor of the courthouse. I had never visited the museum, so
that sounded like a place to start when beginning my next round of
investigation. Cecilia shared how many older files had been destroyed by
the 1939 fire or the occasional flooding of the basement storage room.
I had never attempted to find any court documents because I was also
aware of those instances. I provided her with a list of names-Bond, Kelly,
Adams, and Morris—the men involved in Granddaddy Green's murder
and their involvement dates. She said when she got some extra time that
she would see if she could come up with something for me from the
museum. Shortly after I left her office, Cecilia made a trip up to the
Museum on the fourth floor of the courthouse.

The very next morning after my visit with her, I received a text from
Cecilia "I found something you might be interested in looking at."

The Research Room of the Greene County Museum

What?!

Oh my!

I got dressed as soon as I possibly could and headed into town to the courthouse. Feeling very apprehensive, I opened the door of Cecelia's office and peeked into her desk area. After greeting me, Cecelia turned right around and retrieved three old-looking folders . . . and in an instant my world was totally blown away by what she held! I stood there in silence, with a feeling I cannot put into words, as she handed me folders that contained answers that I had longed to find—court case file folders from the Piney Woods Creek murder cases of 1921. The circuit clerk explained to me that when venturing up to the fourth-floor museum, she first looked through the research room. Next, she carefully inspected a file cabinet sitting just outside in the hallway, and, low and behold, there were the court folders: Case 967: State v Henry A Bond, Case 967: State v John Adams, and Case 969: State v Will Morris et al.

As I looked through teary eyes at each of the folders, I was overwhelmed with emotion as I held a small piece of Green family and Greene County history in my hands. These weathered, yellowed cardboard cases contained some of the original Case Files for the trials of the

Three court case folders from the Piney Woods Creek murders

men indicted for Granddaddy Green's murder. Time and circumstance could have destroyed these precious documents, yet here I stood, blessed to hold them.

The Lord was shining on me that early Tuesday morning. I sat down at a desk in the corner of the Circuit Court Clerk's Office, read through every page and side note, and used my iPad to photograph each page. I was soaking in their treasured contents like I was witnessing the events in person. My eyes were beholding my family's missing history that I thought was lost or destroyed.

Carefully, I took each page from the lightly tattered case file folder and laid it gently before me. Some documents were typewritten, while others had been handwritten in pencil. On one piece of old notebook paper was written in pencil "We the jury find the defendant . . ." just as it had been held in Judge Fatheree's hand in the first of the trials that began in May of 1921. I felt like time stood still within the walls of Cecelia's office and that somehow, I was transported back to that fateful spring of 1921. I could see the jurors in the jury room determining the fate of each man involved. Even if I did not agree with the decisions they made, I would document the results. Each document in those three folders allowed me to gain more insight into the reasoning behind the court system at that time and how each of the individuals involved in the Piney Woods Creek murders was addressed by the court.

Touching my family's history in the Greene County Museum

As I completed the task of taking a picture of each page from each folder, I returned them, oh so carefully, to their home within their assigned folders. I knew I would soon be visiting the Greene County Museum myself, hopefully, to uncover even more treasures from the past.

Leaving the Circuit Clerk's office, I clutched my iPad tightly and held it close to me, as it now held pages of my family's history book. If not for Cecilia's contributions of time and effort, I would have never known these vital documents existed. I left some of the small pieces of the big puzzle in good hands.

Thank you, Cecilia. God puts us in the right places at the right time. He did it again.

CHAPTER TWENTY-FOUR

Searching for Dunnam Clues

I VISITED the Richton Police Department in 2016 to see if anyone there knew anything about the 1921 murders. Officer Bunch and Donna Shipley were the two employees in the office, but neither had ever heard of the Still Raid Murders. So, I decided to seek information elsewhere. I informed Donna about what I was trying to do, and she agreed to help however she could. I then asked for directions to Sunset Cemetery in Richton because I wanted a picture of Lawrence Dunnam's gravesite (one of the items on my bucket list of paraphernalia needed to solve my missing links with all individuals involved in the Still Raid Murders). Officer Bunch offered to allow me to follow him from the police department headquarters to the cemetery.

Arriving at Sunset Cemetery, I began the search for Dunnam's grave. I walked through the cemetery grounds and took pictures of any monument with Dunnam in the name. I then found:

- W.L. Dunnam
- Maggie L./ wife of WL Dunnam, died Jan. 28, 1910 Age 24
- Lizzie Dunnam / January 9, 1893 / Nov. 1911(wife #2) Age 18
- Nettie Dunnam (Jeffcoat) #3 wife (she married a Jeffcoat after Dunnam's death)

I knew I had located William Lawrence's grave, but the others with Dunnam surnames would need more research. I took pictures of the gravestones.

After leaving the Sunset Cemetery, I went by *The Richton Dispatch* newspaper office to see if they had copies of papers from 1921. They said they did not keep any in the office but knew some might be saved on microfilm in the University of Southern Mississippi (USM) library in nearby Hattiesburg. Climbing back into my car, I decided to take another chance and make the fifty-mile drive.

Once on campus, I found parking and went to the McCain Library and Archives, one of the university's libraries. Upon reaching the second floor and with the assistance of a helpful staff member, I uncovered microfilm of *The Richton Dispatch* copies from 1921, 1922, and 1923. It was like finding a nugget of gold on my treasure hunt. Answers to unsolved questions were revealed. Delightedly, I sat for hours and read and copied my prized discoveries. I returned one other day with my daughter Paige, who helped me ensure I had gained all I could from this treasure chest of historical confirmations in the USM Library.

My collection of newspaper articles multiplied with each passing day. I had accumulated more morsels of information and added them to my binders, filling in more missing links related to the officers' deaths.

These snapshots of times past were slowly filling the gap between then and now.

❖ ❖ ❖

After looking on Ancestry.com and Findagrave.com websites in all my research, I hoped to gain as much knowledge about each man involved with Granddaddy Green's death. I wanted to acquire a picture of each individual, gravesite, and individual signatures and determine if they served their sentence. While researching Lawrence Dunnam's family and trying to find a family connection, I found Willye Dunnam McLain's obituary on the Find a Grave Website. Lawrence's wife was six months pregnant in April of 1921, and Willye was the unborn child Nettie was carrying at the time of her husband's death. The daughter was named for her dad, William Lawrence Dunnam.

When I found her obituary on the site, it listed two sons as survivors, Mike and Morgan. I then paid $1.95 to the online source, Spokeo.com, to get the addresses and phone numbers of these two men. Willye's sons were still living, one in Texas and the other in Alabama. The youngest was Morgan, who lived within an hour's drive of my residence in Greene County. I hoped to make a connection.

A few days later, one Sunday afternoon, I tried the number listed for Morgan McLain, as I was curious to know if it was still active. As I took a deep breath, a man answered the phone, and I asked if he was Morgan McLain.

He said, "Yes, ma'am, that's me."

I introduced myself and told him we had something in common-our grandfathers ended their watch as law enforcement officers together on April 1, 1921. He was thrilled to talk with me about something neither of us had been allowed to discuss by our families. Morgan and I spoke for about thirty minutes. Then I asked if I could talk with him in person and bring my research for him to see. We planned the meeting for two days later.

My oldest sister, Debbie, and I made the trek to the McLain home in Mobile, Alabama where we met Morgan McLain and his wife, Bessie. They are two of the sweetest people you will ever meet. It was like a family reunion. Morgan shared several family pictures and a nice one of his grandfather, Lawrence. He then brought out a copper-colored piece in his hand that was Dunnam's constable badge.

Dunnam's badge shared with me by his grandson, Morgan McLain

Missing pieces were coming together. Could it get any better?

Then, Bessie shared that she grew up in the neighborhood where the killings occurred. She shared a story that her father had told her. He said that when he was twelve years old, his father got him to help drive their mule and wagon into the deep Piney Woods to retrieve the bodies of the two murdered officers. They then arranged for the bodies to be transported to the Dunnam home. Their names were John B. and Edward Browder.

Here I was in the living room of the youngest child of Lawrence Dunnam, and then his wife shared such a piece of direct historical connection to Green and Dunnam's death. Bessie also shared that she remembered Mrs. Kelly and two of her daughters visiting their old homeplace when she was little. The Browders purchased the Kelly homeplace after Mancy died, and Bessie had lived in the house growing up.

Since I was a cousin, I asked Morgan if I could represent the Lawrence Dunnam family in connection with completing an application to get the marshal recognized in Washington at the National Law Enforcement Memorial.

With his permission, I was off with my newfound information to pursue yet another journey.

CHAPTER TWENTY-FIVE

Visiting the Still Site

APRIL 1, 2016, was drawing near. The journey back to 1921 was about to unfold again. Most years, on April Fool's Day, I would take my thoughts back to Piney Woods Creek and wonder precisely where Granddaddy Green had been murdered. Considering all I had discovered about his death, I decided to call Mr. David, the good friend of Mancy Kelly's nephew, and see if he could connect me with the Nicholson man who owned the property where the murders were to have taken place. When I reached Mr. David by phone that March morning, he said he would call Kevin and see if I could visit the site on April 1.

Checking the calendar, I discovered that April Fool's Day would fall on a Friday this year. Wouldn't it be amazing if I could arrange a visit ninety-five years later and on the same day of the week as it all happened? It wasn't but a few minutes, and Mr. David called me back and shared Kevin Nicholson's contact information with me. He said Kevin would not mind a bit if I contacted him. I explained my request. He said a visit to the property on Friday, April 1, would not be a problem. Due to the nature of his work as the owner of a logging company, Kevin said weather might be an issue, but for me to plan on coming.

I originally invited my siblings and some cousins to join me. Wiggle's son, Jim, would come from Hattiesburg, and cousins Mark and Sherye Green would drive down from Jackson. The weather for the week of the visit was unfavorable, with severe thunderstorms predicted for Friday. So, on that Wednesday, I called Kevin to let him know that I would have to reschedule the site visit but asked if it was okay with him if I came on Friday to the field by the woods closest to the creek and parked my truck to work on the book I was writing.

He then made a surprising offer! He asked what I was doing then, and I told him I was at home with no plans. He said if I could drive over, he would show me where to go, and I could come back anytime I wanted to take other family members to the still site.

I quickly ran outside to where Andy was working in his barn and asked him whether he minded if I went to Richton to meet with Kevin.

He said, "Go for it!"

So that's what I did.

Was it crazy to be going to meet this man, a total stranger, and travel into the woods with him? God was right there beside me all the way. I drove to Kevin's shop and logging maintenance garage at his parents' home. His property bordered Piney Woods Creek. Once I parked my truck and stepped out, he welcomed me and asked if my vehicle had a four-wheel drive.

I said, "No."

He then said we would need to take his truck across the field in case we got bogged down in the wet grass. So off I go, getting into a truck with a stranger to trek into the woods, looking for the area where my grandfather's murder took place.

I took my iPad to record our journey. I did most of the talking as we traveled to the edge of the field and entered a pathway into the wooded area closest to the creek. I explained the history of the murders to Kevin as I followed him into the woods. In a few minutes, it seemed as if the present had slipped away, as now I was in a place where years of investigating and pondering about what had happened was in front of me—an area of his property on which was spread around parts and pieces of a broken-up moonshine still.

All I could say, over and over, was, "Wow!"

As we walked through the site of the abandoned still, Kevin told me that he had played in these woods as a boy and shared with me stories of some of the relics he had discovered left behind through the years

Components of a moonshine still

by bootleggers. Although remains of the still before us had some post-1921 parts, evidence that someone had used it years after the murders, it was incredibly overwhelming to be standing on the property where Granddaddy Green had died! Kevin allowed me to bring home some souvenirs that day. I chose a small pot with holes shot through it and several pieces of glass moonshine jugs.

Once we arrived back at his shop, Kevin even gave me a full unbroken jug that he had recovered from the site while a teenager. He shared how he had made some wine and stored it in the jug. He graciously informed me that I was welcome anytime to bring others to visit the site without his having to be there.

Are you kidding me? That's what I call Southern Mississippi Hospitality!

Andy, our children, and my siblings were dumbfounded when I returned home and shared my serendipitous experience. I told them I would return on Friday morning, the first, around ten a.m., to sit in the field and work on my writing, come rain or shine. I shared Kevin's hospitality and contemplated rescheduling the site visit. Well, you have to know my family: they all wanted to come join me. So, I told them to be there by ten, and we would sit in our vehicles and honor Granddaddy Green on the ninety-fifth anniversary of his death.

But God had another ending to this saga.

The prediction for heavy thunderstorms at daybreak on Friday morning was 100 percent. Despite the dreadful-looking sky, I was off to Richton in my truck. Andy would meet me there at the appointed time, along with my sisters, Debbie and Lisa, and cousins Jim, Mark, and Sherye. Even though my anxiety was rising due to the expected bad weather, a sense of peace washed over me, one that assured me I did not need to check the hour-to-hour weather app and that all was going to be okay. I followed that intuition.

When I pulled up at Kevin's place, clouds were low and heavy, but the severe weather had stalled. Everyone in our party arrived, and we headed to the still site before the storm began. We were dressed both for

Jake Green's descendants visit the site of the Piney Woods Creek Murders of 1921

mosquito attacks and an approaching downpour. With me was a short historical overview to share and some memorial items I planned to leave at the site.

Although I led the group to where I thought Kevin had taken me earlier that week, Andy had to venture out and find the hidden area I had somehow missed. Silence prevailed for the first few minutes as we approached the still site. Tears streamed down several cheeks. Few words were spoken. I shared my short overview, and we took pictures. Some gathered a few relics, as Kevin graciously allowed us to bring them home as remembrances.

So, here we were honoring Granddaddy Green exactly ninety-five years after he lost his life on the banks of Piney Woods Creek while raiding a still like the one we were standing in the midst of.

As I had pondered several times in recent years of my research, "Could God bless me anymore?"

April Fool's Day 2016.

He did it once again.

As we made our way out of the mosquito-infested swampland, a gentle rain began to fall. God had held back the storm to allow our Green family to pay tribute to our historical icon, my Granddaddy Green.

Amazing!

PART V

Valor Forever Reigns

"Even the bravest that are slain shall not
dissemble their surprise on
waking to find valor reign."

—Robert Frost, Inscription on the
ATF Fallen Officer's Memorial Wall in
Washington, D.C.

My Mississippi Men

I N the spring of 2011, members of two Greene County families were invited to attend a memorial service honoring officers who died in the line of duty. Both of the men honored—Special Agent Jake Green of the Bureau of Alcohol, Tobacco, Firearms and Explosives and Deputy Sheriff Murdock McIntosh of the Greene County Sheriff's Department—were murdered in the 1920s but had never been appropriately memorialized in Greene County for their loss of life while fulfilling duties as law enforcement officers.

Three years after Granddaddy Green's death, the notorious outlaw, Kennie Wagner, murdered McIntosh on December 24, 1924, when the Greene County Deputy Sheriff attempted to arrest Wagner at a local residence where he was hiding out.[1] Wagner fired several times, striking the Greene County officer and fatally wounding him.[2] McIntosh and Green would have known each other, as McIntosh served as a Deputy Sheriff in 1921 when Granddaddy and Marshal Dunnam were killed raiding the still.

Sheriff Kevin Fortinberry and his wife, Scharlotte, coordinated the ceremony held on Wednesday, May 11, 2011, at McLeod-Magnolia Cemetery in Leakesville, where both men were buried. Representatives of both families and other law enforcement officers from Greene County were in attendance. A U.S. flag, folded appropriately, was presented to each family during the ceremony. "Taps" was played, followed by a three-volley gun salute. Surprisingly, the service was a very emotional

Green family members honor Jake's sacrifice: (from left to right) Byron Green, Jr., Billy Green, Jake Green, Lisa Green Hedegaard, Debbie Green McLeod, Juanita Green Hollinghead, and Jim Green

event, despite the time that had passed and that no one in attendance was around during the decade in which these two men were killed.

Having both officers honored at the ceremony was one type of closure for both families.

Both the Green and McIntosh families attended Leakesville United Methodist Church. My dad, Polly Green, and McIntosh's son, Farve—both sons of the fallen officers—grew up in that church environment and brought their families up there, too. Common connections were never discussed by either survivor who grew up fatherless because certain individuals thought themselves above the law.

In that same year, 2011, McIntosh's family worked with the Greene County Sheriff's Department to have his name added to the National Law Enforcement Officers Memorial wall (NLEOM) in our nation's capital. The story made front-page news in our local paper, *The Greene County Herald*. The article detailed the family's efforts to honor McIntosh's selfless service. As I read the piece, I thought, *Why not my granddaddy?*

❖ ❖ ❖

Three years later, I began my campaign to make sure my grandfather's name was also on the memorial wall in Washington. When I first talked by phone with Carolie Heyliger from the National Law Enforcement Officers Memorial in Washington in September of 2015, I requested information about getting fallen officers recognized. She advised me that it was best to have family members work with the agencies where the officers were employed because they had to confirm certain obligations to complete the paperwork. I had already been diligently working to locate family members from all men involved in the Still Raid. I scoured various online databases, including Find a Grave, Google, and Spokeo, and conducted in-person interviews to glean anything I could about all the individuals involved. I had already made some connections with relatives of Marshal Lawrence Dunnam and jailer Russ Harris. Another name to add was that of B.M. Millstead, another Marshal from Richton, who was murdered the year before the incident at Piney Woods Creek.

Time crept by as I waited to receive information and applications for the officers. I wondered why Carolie had not mentioned anything about my grandfather's application. The other three men's paperwork arrived in my mailbox, but there was none for Granddaddy Green. I knew I would need to get details from the ATF.

While on a subsequent call with Carolie, I mentioned not getting an application for my grandfather's recognition. What she said next almost knocked me out of my chair—Jacob F. Green's name was already on the NLEOM wall and had been in the inaugural group of officers listed when the wall was first erected. I was stunned!

As soon as I hung up with Carolie, I immediately called the Bureau of Alcohol, Tobacco, Firearms and Explosives (ATF) to find out more details about submitting Jake's name. I was delighted to confirm that the ATF had already submitted Granddaddy's name in 1989 as one of their fallen agents. Due to the destruction of his personnel file in an office fire, there was no family information for the agency to use to notify our family. Jake's name had been on the wall since its beginning. How bittersweet.

Dunnam's grandson, Morgan McLain, and Harris' great niece, Judith Wallace, permitted me to pursue the application process for their family members. I assured them that I would keep them informed about what I learned. I would have to convince each officer's agency to complete the application process and forward it to Washington.

After getting permission to represent the Dunnam family, I then visited Richton Police Headquarters for the second time. I had a feeling that Chief Gardner had the paperwork the office in Washington had sent him but might still need to fill it out. After introducing myself to him, I told the chief why I was there. As I was talking, Chief Gardner reached down to his left side, opened a drawer of his office desk, and pulled out a packet of paperwork that contained not one but two applications!

Both Dunnam's and Millstead's NLEOM applications were in the jacket. I told the chief that I knew little about Millstead except what I read in a newspaper clipping that I had sent to show proof of Dunnam's death in my request. I told Chief Gardner what I already knew about Dunnam and promised to complete some research on Millstead. Our collaboration would get both men recognized in Washington. Next, the chief called Donna, his secretary, into his office and asked her to assist me in filing the paperwork. I told her that I would do whatever was needed.

A few weeks passed, and when I did not hear anything from the Richton Police Department, I checked in with Donna. She shared that she needed help answering several application questions, and I immediately gave her Carolie's contact information. A few days later, Donna called back to say she had completed all the paperwork and sent the documents to Washington. We would make the December 31st deadline. Two down and one to go!

In October of 2016, I was watching Greene County play a football game at Purvis. While there, I received a cell phone call from Carolie, telling me that the NLEOM Board of Directors had approved Dunnam's and Millstead's names at its recent meeting. She apologized for the odd time of night to be calling but said she knew I would be anxious to find out. Before ending the call, Carolie told me that the invitations to the ceremonies would soon be sent and that she needed me to compile a list of survivors from each of the two men's families so that they would receive invitations to the ceremony in May.

Now that those two names were approved, I only had two months until the end-of-the-year deadline to try to get Jailer Harris's family contacted. I needed the help of the Hinds County Sheriff in order to complete the application and send it on to Washington. My prayer was that the paperwork would get approved for Harris's name to be added to the memorial wall in May of 2017.

The next day I contacted Morgan McLain and Pat Holland Hyde, two of Lawrence Dunnam's grandchildren, to inform them of their grandfather's acceptance.

On Saturday, October 29, I received two letters from the NLEOM. One was confirmation of Dunnam's approval, and the second was for Millstead. It was an emotional experience as I opened this long-awaited correspondence, as if blessing after blessing were now being poured out on my journey to get all these fallen officers honored.

Completing Harris' application for the NLEOM was a different story. When I had made connections through Find a Grave with his great-niece, Judith Wallace, she was very helpful and offered to go with me to the Hinds County Sheriff to request his assistance. She also shared a twenty-page research paper she had written in 1984 about her uncle's death in 1922. The paper included several newspaper articles I did not have; I added them to my stash.

The NLEOM sent Harris's application paperwork to the Hinds County Sheriff's Department and the Richton Police Department but with no response. I concluded that his application had been shuffled around, as did the paperwork in Richton the previous November. Meanwhile, I investigated the Hinds County Sheriff's Department website and found the glitch that most likely caused a delay. The first was that the department had no clue who Russell Harris was and did not pursue the application. The next nugget of information I discovered would make more sense and have a more straightforward solution.

It had been an election year when the application arrived, and a new sheriff was now in office. I called newly elected Sheriff Victor Mason and left a message, and he returned my call a few days later. I explained that he could be the missing link to help get this officer recognized nationally on the NLEOM Wall. He vowed to do whatever he could to help expedite the matter.

The easiest way was for me to fill out the application and fax it to Sheriff Mason, have him sign it, and then send it directly to Washington. Chancery Clerk Shelley Eubanks helped with this step. She faxed the documents, he signed them, and returned them by fax to her. I made copies and sent Harris's application by mail before the December 31st deadline. I took a hiatus and hoped Harris would make the list of the names to be added in 2017, as my other Mississippi Men—law enforcement officials from my home state who had died in the line of duty as related to my grandfather's death. I had completed the last of the three new Mississippi Men's applications. With the approval of Harris's application in February of 2017, there were now four fallen officers from Mississippi: Green, Dunnam, Harris, and Millstead, who became known as My Mississippi Men.

I would now need to get a list of family members of each man and retrieve emails and addresses so they could receive an official survivor's invitation to the ceremony. To reach a broad audience quickly, I wrote an article for the *Greene County Herald* and *The Richton Dispatch* requesting names of these men's families.

Plans were made for the trip to Washington to go see, for the first time, my Granddaddy's name on the NLEOM wall and to hear the names of "My Mississippi Men" announced at the 29th Annual Candlelight Vigil recognition ceremony held on the National Mall on May 13, 2017. My sister, Debbie, made the trek with me, and we agreed that the experience was one of the most emotional and moving events we have ever experienced. How happy I was to travel to Washington to honor and represent these men, so dear to my heart, as well as every other name on the wall.

It was very peaceful as we visited the NLEOM Wall for the first time early one morning, when the visitors were few. I had with me the panel and number for locating each officer's name. I created nametags and red-rose arrangements for each one. In my memorial acknowledgments, I included Greene County's Deputy Murdock McIntosh and George County Sheriff Garry Welford. My Mississippi Men binge became

Here to honor My Mississippi Men

recognition honors for Green, Dunnam, Millstead, and Harris. I even created a Memorial Backpack with all the men's names to transport my rose arrangements. McIntosh and Welford were two other officers with

Debbie and me touching Jake's name on the NLEOM wall

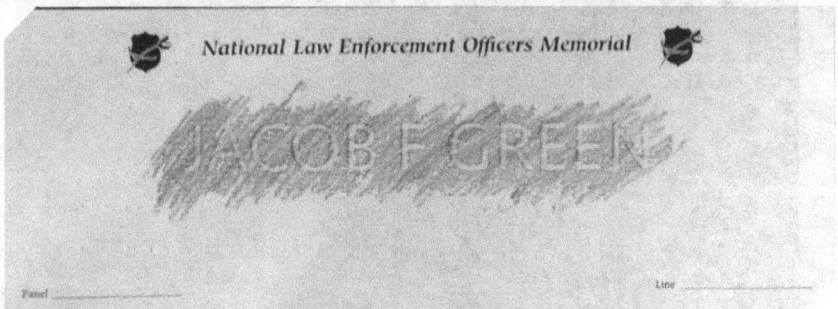

My rubbing of Granddaddy Green's name on the NLEOM wall

family connections I wanted to recognize on the wall. Debbie and I made pencil rubbings of each officer's engraved name.

As the "My Mississippi Men" survivors, Debbie, her son, Benji, and his wife, Mollie, and I entered the event arena that Saturday evening. My nephew and his wife, who were living in Pennsylvania, had driven over to join us for the ceremony. Active law enforcement officers then escorted us to specially reserved seats. My police escort handed me a survivor rose, and she solemnly listened to the story of "My Mississippi Men" as we wove our way through the officer-bordered passageway to my assigned seat on the south lawn of the National Mall. As I sat down and looked forward, I faced our nation's capital.

There was a screen up, showing pictures of the 394 men and women to be recognized during the candlelight vigil. After completion of the Roll Call of Officers, we lit memorial candles. I had requested that my grandfather's name be called out with those of the new inductees but discovered it was too late to honor that request. As each state's representatives approached the podium, each officer's survivors would stand up.

I was overwhelmed with a rollercoaster of emotions as the name of the state of Mississippi was soon to be announced. I would proudly stand

The headstone of the Green Widow: Eliza Roberts Green, with survivor rose

169

up for all My Mississippi Men, but I would verbalize my granddaddy's name if the committee chose not to add it to this year's newest Mississippi names announced.

An officer read the following statement, "For the State of Mississippi, John Russell Harris, James Lee Tart, B. M. Millstead, William Lawrence Dunnam, Clarence James Lanier." A bell solemnly sounded. Quietly, I whispered, "Jacob F. Green." As I uttered my granddaddy's name, it was as if all the emotions I had buried deep within myself were released, and a door closed, signifying the end of a very, very long journey of my life. God did it again.

Upon returning home to Leakesville, Mississippi, I needed to make one last stop on my journey. One that would make it come full circle. As I entered McLeod-Magnolia Cemetery through the front archway and turned right toward the Green family plot, I felt surreal, knowing I was where I needed to be on that day. As I parked the car, I thanked the Lord for all of His help throughout my pursuit of this quest and its fruitful conclusion.

I had returned from my Washington trip with several pieces of memorabilia: a stain-glassed cross and rose arrangement that had adorned Granddaddy Green's name on the wall in Washington, several small United States flags, and my survivor rose that I carried during the ceremony. Carefully, I pulled each item from My Mississippi Men's backpack. I placed four small United States flags at the base of his headstone. I then carefully removed from the bag the cross arrangement I had made to be displayed close to his name in Washington and secured it in the middle. Finally, I retrieved the rose with a blue ribbon that was given to me as a survivor of a fallen officer at the ceremony in Washington.

As I secured the rose's stem into the ground before her grave monument, I deemed Eliza Roberts Green the Ultimate Survivor. She stayed faithful to Jake even after his death. She was his Forever Love.

This journey of remembrance was now at its end, as that rose represented all the survivors of Special Agent Jacob F. Green: End of Watch, April 1, 1921.

CHAPTER TWENTY-SEVEN

The Centennial

URING the COVID-19 Pandemic in 2020, my cousin, Mark Green, contacted me. For many years, he assisted me and participated in my quest to gather more historical information about our Green family. Mark and his wife, Sherye, share my passion for and love of history. Jake's great-nephew knew of my desire to memorialize Granddaddy Green's sacrifice and did not want this important event in our state's history to go unnoticed. During his call, Mark told me he had made some inquiries into what it would take to get a Mississippi Department of Archives and History (MDAH) historical marker placed near the site of the Still Raid Murders of 1921. Upon his recommendation that MDAH would most likely be on board with such a request, Mark forwarded the department's contact information, including the application process. I immediately went to work.

As I pursued this as the ultimate ending to my journey of memorializing Granddaddy Green, I included research I conducted on Officer Lawrence Dunnam in the application process. Jim Woodrick, a historian at the MDAH, became our liaison for the project. He was confident that this historical marker would become a reality from the start. Although he was soon to retire, Jim promised to stay connected with me to get this done, since one of the department's requirements was to have local officials' support as part of the application requirements and support from local legislators.

After talking to my Mississippi State Senator, Dennis DeBar, I decided to submit a two-fold request. Besides the historical marker, I also requested that a section of Highway 42 between Sand Hill and the Greene-Perry County Line be renamed for the officers as a Memorial Highway. Senator DeBar advised me to get a unanimous resolution from the Greene County Board of Supervisors (BOS). Once secured, he would introduce a bill to make it happen.

I then requested to be placed on the agenda for the Greene County BOS meeting the first week of April. I attended the board meeting with a written proposal, where the document was discussed and approved. A final version was prepared and forwarded to Jackson to begin making its way through the legislative process. Senator Debar and Representative Dale Goodin championed my efforts to have the highway sign completed and installed before the one-hundred-year celebration planned for April 1, 2021.

The application for the historical marker went to the MDAH in the third week of April of 2020. The Polly Wiggle Joy Corporation and the Green family would take responsibility for private funding of the historical marker, but the Dunnam family also graciously contributed funds. True to his word, Jim Woodrick helped me complete the application for the historical marker. Once the board approved the request at the end of October of 2020, the order for the historical signage was placed.

House Bill (HB) 1279 passed on July 25, 2020, and I thought all was well. However, in September, when I reached out to Senator Debar about the Centennial celebration, he told me that even though the newly enacted legislation contained an original version of the resolution, the word count needed to be shorter to fit onto a roadside plaque.

With the assistance of Krista Guice from the Mississippi Department of Transportation (MDOT), we reduced the wording. The Greene County BOS also agreed to issue a resolution revision to accommodate the wording change.

As I shared details of the celebration event with her, Krista reminded me that MDOT would not conduct an official ceremony due to COVID-19 guidelines. Her expertise was enormously beneficial in planning the agenda and setting the protocol for a signage dedication ceremony. I told her that we would commemorate the lives of Green and Dunnam on April 1, 2021, whether state officials could be there or not. She assured me that she would keep me informed about who from MDOT might be able to attend.

A few months later, in January, Senator DeBar returned to the state legislature with the revision to HB 1279 and added changes to include in Senate Bill (SB) 2481. By the end of February of 2021, SB 2481 went through the proper channels and became law. Well, I thought we had cleared all legislative hurdles! I was disappointed to learn from Krista that the creation of signage covered under any law passed in the 2021 legislative session would go into effect on July 1, 2021. I had hoped to have the historical marker completed and installed for the centennial. Krista said she would have a mock sign designed for the ceremony and that MDOT would install the real one in July.

Legislators DeBar and Goodin changed the wording on the paperwork to read "effective immediately." It then had to go back to be voted upon through the legislative process. The stroke of their pens cleared the last hurdle for creating and placing the highway memorial sign. These two men were such a blessing throughout the process.

When I approached him, Pastor Nick Chatham of First Baptist Church Sand Hill graciously agreed to allow us to use their fellowship hall and said church members would be honored to have the ceremony held there. The event would begin at 10:00 A.M. on April 1st, the exact time Green and Dunnam would have been planning their raid of the still on Piney Woods Creek. Everything was coming together, with many volunteers helping to pull it off.

One hundred years later, to the day and the time of the dreaded event, close to one hundred well-wishers gathered on the morning of April 1, 2021, for a ceremony to memorialize these officers. Members of both the Green and Dunnam families and close friends of both joined representatives of various local, state, and federal law enforcement agencies, including agents from the Bureau of Alcohol, Tobacco, Firearms and Explosives.

After the ceremony at the church, guests visited both memorial signs that were placed in Greene County to honor and remember the

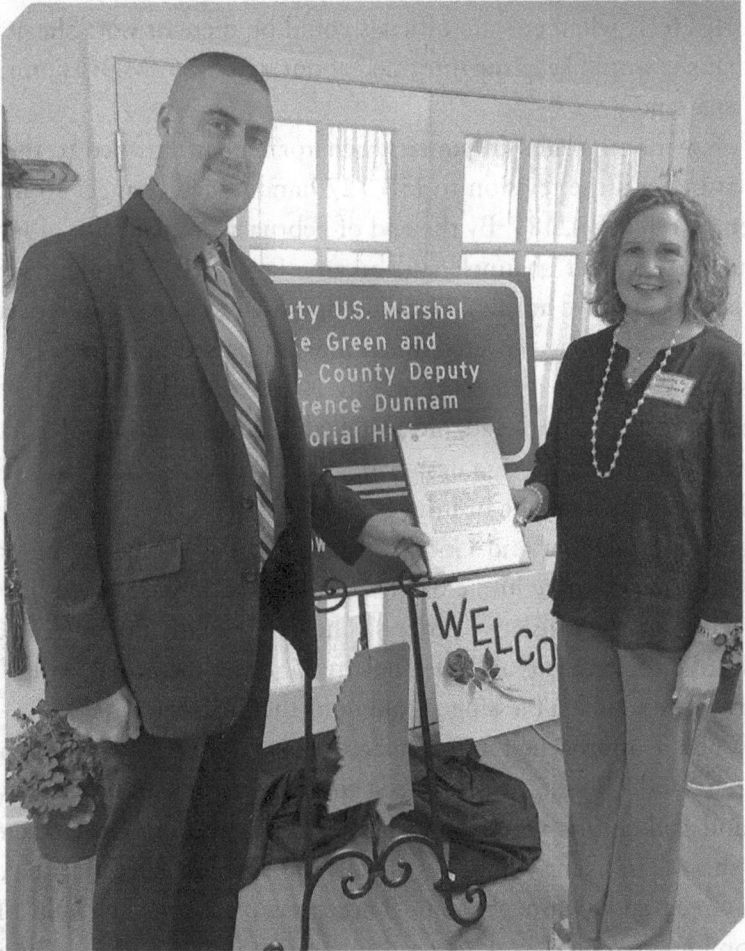

ATF Officer Jason Denham presents letter from acting ATF Director to Jake's granddaughter, Juanita Green Hollinghead (photo courtesy of Bureau of Alcohol, Tobacco, Firearms and Explosives)

sacrifices of Agent Jake Green and Marshal Lawrence Dunnam. The first was the historical marker from the Mississippi Department of Archives and History near the bridge over Piney Woods Creek. The second was a memorial highway sign announcing the renaming of a portion of Highway 42, right inside the Greene/Perry County Line, to the intersection in Sand Hill that heads towards Leakesville.

Memorial highway marker

Still Raid Murders MDAH marker

My grandfather Jake Green and Mr. Lawrence Dunnam would have perhaps thought it strange that so many gathered that morning to make a fuss over their lives, as they were two men who died the way they lived—giving their best for their family and their country every day, never expecting any thanks in return.

May their ultimate sacrifice and legacy of selfless service continue through each of us, the living.

CHAPTER TWENTY-EIGHT

Never Forgotten

ADDING Jake's name to the Wall of Mississippi's Fallen Officers in Jackson, Mississippi, would be the last strand woven into my Green Widow's web. I visited the wall in 2017 to find all My Mississippi Men's names newly engraved for that year. As is the protocol for the National Law Enforcement Officers Memorial (NLEOM), Mississippi adds the names of those added each year in Washington to the state wall erected in 1991 to pay tribute to Mississippi's fallen officers. Each program has guidelines for selection, and names added to the national memorial are automatically added to the one in Jackson the same year.

When I returned from my 2017 trip to Washington, I visited Jackson to peek at the newly added names. Though I searched for Granddaddy Green's name, his was not there! Of course, I knew I needed to find out why not. I triple-checked to ensure I had not missed it, but it was nowhere to be found on that granite wall. I hoped this visit to the Jackson wall would bring closure for me, but I felt a critical strand would be missing from the web without adding his name. Jake deserved to be honored along with the others in his home state, which he was so proud to be a part of. The same sense of pride and respect instilled in me kept me from retiring my investigator's badge. I promised Andy and myself that this would be the last addition to my long list of chronological events related to Granddaddy Green's death. God had a few more surprises in store for me, and it wasn't until the fall of 2020 that this last strand began its construction.

In April of 2020, work began on a double signage ceremony honoring Green and Dunnam scheduled for April 1, 2021, the one-hundredth-year anniversary of their murders. 2020 became the year of planning the last events on my "to-do list." During a hectic stretch of that year, I took a break and searched for the right person to assist in getting Granddaddy Green's name added to the Mississippi wall. I sought out different websites to see who sponsored the wall. After a diligent search, I contacted the president of the Mississippi Association of Chiefs of Police and called him to get some answers. He advised me to contact Robert Davis, an association member who took care of adding names to the memorial.

I was blessed when I finally got Robert on the phone. I told him my dilemma about Granddaddy Green's name not being on the wall. He shared that information for the wall came from Washington, and if names were included on the NLEOM wall, they were automatically added to the Mississippi wall. As we continued to talk, he pulled up the NLEOM website and told me that he could see the name of Jacob F. Green on that national monument. He said that was all the confirmation he needed and that Granddaddy's name would be engraved sometime in April, before Police Week in May.

Juanita (left), Lisa (center), and Debbie (right) at the Mississippi Fallen Officers Memorial Wall

Could God be any more incredible?

After the signage ceremony in April, we would look forward to the ceremony in May to see Jake's name come home to Mississippi and be honored as it should. Two weeks after the centennial celebration, Robert emailed to notify us that my grandfather's name had been placed on the monument on April 12, 2021. This gracious man even took pictures of the wall and a close-up of the panel where the name of Jacob F. Green was located and shared them with me.

God did it again, like so many times through my travels on this journey of the unknown unveiled.

Tuesday, May 18, 2021, was the 2021 Mississippi Fallen Officers Candlelight Vigil at the Fallen Officers Memorial Wall in Jackson, Mississippi, a ceremony now delayed a week due to severe weather. Members of the Jacob F. Green family received invitations to attend. With great excitement, Andy and I headed to Jackson early that morning. We were to meet William "Brother" Rogers to tour a special exhibit on Prohibition soon to close at the Museum of Mississippi History.

A visit to the Two Mississippi Museums complex was a bonus that I am so glad I got to experience. So much of the Prohibition exhibit's information was familiar to me because the research of that period in American history was part of my investigation. One highlight of our visit was making a short video about Green and Dunnam in the recording booth area. Other visitors to the special exhibit could now hear a forty-five-second glimpse into my family's world of moonshine.

Earlier that spring, I had received an inquiry from the Mississippi Department of Archives and History to ask if I would consider donating any of the items related to the raid on Piney Woods Creek. Our family unanimously agreed to the request, and we made plans for me to return at a future date to deliver them to the department staff. The contents of the spider's sack, the leather satchel, and Granddaddy's hat he was wearing would now become part of a permanent collection at the archives. The Dunnam family also agreed to donate Lawrence's constable badges and some family pictures.

As evening approached on that Tuesday, rain clouds hovered over Jackson. Andy and I sat in the truck before it was time to venture toward the ceremony site. Suddenly, a blur of activity captured our attention. Several motorcycle officers rode past as they practiced their route to the event. From where we sat, we could see many more preparations underway. Finally, the time arrived, and we walked over to the lawn between the Carroll Gartin Justice Building and the Walter Sillers State Office Building. Finding our way to the tent reserved for the survivors, we took our seats. We arrived just in the nick of time, as the storm clouds delivered a heavy downpour with strong gusts of wind. My cousin, Cindy

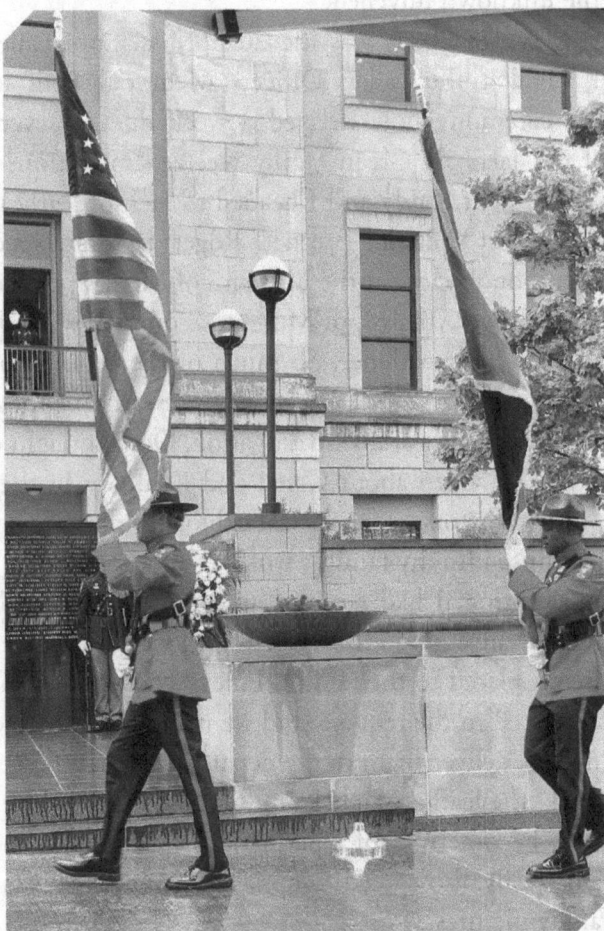

Ceremony at the Mississippi Fallen Officers Memorial Wall

Brunson, braved the weather and joined us under the tent to honor her great-uncle, Jake.

Though the Attorney General did her best as the event host, only a few remarks could be heard above the storm. The wind and rain muffled the singing and speeches of the ceremony, but none of that mattered to me—my eyes were fixed on a stone bowl sitting to the right of the wall, brimming with beautiful red roses. There was one with Granddaddy Green's name on it, and it would soon be in my hands. When the presentation of the 2021 additions to the wall started, I listened closely through the pouring rain.

The candlelight vigil turned into a presentation of roses due to the downpour. If survivors chose to present the roses at the base of the wall, closest to the officer's engraved name, they would come forward as their family member's name was called. The very first name called was Jacob F. Green, Department of Alcohol, Tobacco, Firearms and Explosives, EOW April 1, 1921. As I stood up, an escort met me, holding his umbrella over me as I walked proudly to my spot, directly under Jake's name. With honor and pride, I carefully placed my survivor rose at the monument's base under Granddaddy Green's name. I touched my lips with my fingertips and gently placed my fingers over his name as if to say, "The end." My face was soaking wet, but not from the raindrops. Tears ran down my cheeks, the tracks of an emotional rollercoaster that had now finally come to the end of the ride. But, oh, what a ride! I would not go back and change one thing along the path of my now complete journey.

The knowledge I gained from every experience, both big and small, will forever be preserved within these pages, so my Granddaddy Green's story will never be forgotten.

Prohibition Agent Jacob F. Green, Sr.
Jan. 3, 1884 – Apr. 1, 1921

Prohibition Special Agent Jake Green (photo courtesy of Bureau of Alcohol, Tobacco, Firearms and Explosives)

Afterword

I FEEL like I've been running a triathlon but have no idea when and where the race began or where its final destination will be. I believe the childhood curiosity of not knowing and not being able to ask about the death of my Granddaddy Green was the starting point of what would erupt into an outpouring of information gained throughout my lifetime. More like a 10,000-piece puzzle, just waiting to be put together.

April Fools' Day became a Memorial Day for me throughout my life. After Daddy passed away in 1988, he took pieces of the puzzle to his grave that I never could regain, but his absence led me down paths I would have never gone. Some parts of the evidence trail, I thought, were destroyed by fire and flood but were left for me to find years later. I often said, "He did it again!" when God would allow me to be at the right place and time to uncover just one more piece of the puzzle. What transpired on this journey was no accident or just luck; it was a God-orchestrated journey that only He knew the final chapter.

I had years of procrastination where I would search for more, but life took me down other paths. Teaching Mississippi History to my fourth and sixth-grade students was one of my favorite seasons throughout my tenure. I would always tell them my Mississippi History story of my grandfather getting killed while raiding a whiskey still in 1921. Each time I shared it, they told me I needed to write a book to tell his story.

A few years before Momma passed away and I was staying home with her, various parts of this complicated story began to be revealed to me.

If God had not allowed me to put my teaching on the back burner to help her, some of the highlighted puzzle pieces would never have crossed my path. Little by little, clues started showing up around me, and the longing to put more time into investigating his story led me to uncover my story, along with his.

The picture created when the pieces came together unveiled Jake's story, and God allowed me to discover more than I ever dreamed and far beyond that fateful day of April 1, 1921. Recognizing Granddaddy Green as a Fallen Officer from Greene County in 2011 was a rekindling spark for me. As I finished my tenure as an educator in the Greene County School System in 2012, I vowed to spend more time searching for more puzzle pieces. I wanted to discover the rest of the story behind the few documents I had uncovered concerning Granddaddy's death.

I searched the World Wide Web for any clues yet hidden, and 2015 was my gold mine year. I became what some might call addicted to researching anything I thought might produce results. I look back now, and it feels as though I've been trying to get this to fruition for an eternity. I often felt exhausted, but then another puzzle piece would be revealed, or I would get a call or email back from someone who would become a piece that made it all worth it. After starting with only a few documents to go on and now having thousands of papers to refer to as justifiable is sometimes overwhelming.

Sometimes, this feeling was hard to explain, but as I held pieces of the past in my hands that allowed me to return to the time and place they originated, it often brought me to tears and sometimes laughter. The best advice I would give my students while reading a book would be to put themselves into a character's place and be that person. Feel what they would have felt and soak up each moment in the character's shadow. That's what I wanted to do with this book, to take you alongside Granddaddy Green during his last days on Earth. You would then follow each character's steps in this deadly plot of selfish pride as you witnessed his death, investigation, and murder trials that followed like you were there.

Next, I wanted to take you with me on my journey as I uncovered piece by piece the stories that transpired beyond April 1, 1921, and allow you to partner with me as I revealed the "beyond" accounts.

It is now time for me to step out of the book and allow you to step in and understand the importance of not letting your family's story stay hidden. To all my students who told me to write a book or asked me, "Have you written that book yet?" I now can say, "With God as my guide, I did it!"

Daddy always taught us to be proud of who we are and where we're from.

He taught us to stand and salute the American flag.

Show respect to your elders.

Always try your best in whatever you attempt.

Family comes first.

Always go to church anytime the doors are open.

Be proud to be an American.

Your word is your best asset.

Give 110 percent in all your work.

God's guidance through this journey was no accident. The encounters I experienced through him allowed me to be in certain places, at certain times, to meet specific individuals and uncover bits and pieces of information that otherwise would have been forgotten by history. God showed up and showed out on my journey to discover the past, so I can share with the present and leave for the future the true legacy of Jake Green, my Granddaddy Green.

Find your story, your sack, or your satchel because every family has one that otherwise might be lost if you don't grasp the moment and start your journey into the past so your future can carry on what could be lost forever.

Acknowledgments

M Y daddy, Jacob "Polly" Francis Green, Jr., needs credit for being my best buddy throughout my childhood until Andy took over that spot. I get my Green-minded stubbornness and persistence from him, and I know those attributes helped me search for clues in places I wasn't allowed when he was living. Thanks, Daddy!

My momma, Ruth, saw positivity in every situation, even when so much negativity surrounded her while on her married life's journey as the Green Widow's closest challenge. She was my best friend in her last days and always encouraged me to keep looking for answers to my lists of questions. She was and continues to be an inspiration as I try to have more Ruth days in my life.

Andy, my husband and childhood sweetheart of over fifty years, started this journey with me as a third-grade classmate, as he always knew I never made any jokes on April Fool's Day. The support of my child-like inquiries throughout our life together has made this challenge of completing the story come to reality—forty-two years of Always and Forever plus More!

Drew and Paige, my offspring, their spouses Elisabeth and Chris, all their spiderlings (Brody, Bella, Raylee, Bethany, Sarah Jane, Nathan, Archer, and Grace), and my "other sons" Keaton and Noah, are a large part of my why. I hope they would feel a closer connection to Granddaddy Green, recognize how important our family history is, and desire to carry that forward in the lives of their own families.

My siblings—Jake Green, Debbie Green McLeod, Lisa Green Hedegaard, and my cousins, Joy Taylor, Jim Green, and the late Billy Green—are all grandchildren of Jake Green. None of them let me, Jake Green's youngest grandchild, off the hook about finishing what I started many years ago.

Lisa is my "thorn-in-the-side" sister, but in a good way—her constant reminders have spurred me to work on the book. My big sister, Debbie, was my cohort on several field trips to explore and discover more information. Sisters make the best of friends.

I commend Joy—my first cousin and closest-to-Mimi connection—for her poignant, literary-minded advice much needed and appreciated.

The late Byron "Little Doc" Green, Jr., my second cousin, for his Green Family History collaboration and for being the historian on his branch of our family tree.

I was so blessed to have God orchestrate a new relationship with my cousin, Sherye. She held my hand and heart throughout this process, and I now call her my friend. She can ride sidesaddle with me on any adventure in the future. We'll let her husband Mark drive!

My deepest gratitude goes to the following individuals for their valuable contributions to my journey:

Lifelong friend Randy Pierce assisted me in several areas throughout the latter years of writing this story. Being a published author, his knowledge of the process helped guide me through some questionable obstacles. It was a blessing for him to honor my request to write the foreword. Greene County roots run deep!

Sunbury Press Publisher Lawrence Knorr and his staff of supportive individuals who worked tirelessly to bring this story to fruition have been such a blessing. Many thanks go out to Publishing Assistant Katie Cressman, Editors Amanda Krieger and Anaya Montgomery, Book Designer Crystal Devine, and Manager of Marketing and Publicity John Jordan for contributions of your time and talents to allow this story to be told.

Morgan McLain, Lawrence Dunnam's grandson, son of Dunnam's youngest child, Willye Dunnam, for multiple contributions, and his wife, Bessie McLain, shared stories of living around the Kelly family.

The late Rufus Walley for his heartfelt apology for his Uncle Mancy killing my Granddaddy Green and his wife, Hazel, for sharing more family history after Rufus's death.

Taylor Meadows Walley helped me reconnect with Hazel Walley at the Distinguished Young Woman's Retreat.

Diane Goodnight, Mancy Kelly's great-niece, provided family history about the Kellys that led to other doors being opened.

David Smith, Rufus Walley's friend, once owned the property on which the murders occurred and provided helpful information about it.

Tiffany Walley Smith, Rufus Walley's granddaughter, reconnected me with him.

Kevin and Cassie Nicholson, present owners of the still site property on Piney Woods Creek, gave visitation rights to Jake Green's extended family members several times.

Rayford Freeman, my son-in-law's step-grandfather, owned property adjacent to Piney Woods Creek and generously shared information about it.

Cecilia Bounds, Greene County Circuit Clerk—for her persistence in locating lost files, which spurred a domino effect of uncovering priceless court documents.

Shelley Eubanks, Greene County Chancery Court Clerk—for assisting me in filing documentation during the application process for the National Law Enforcement Officer's Memorial (NLEOM) recognition.

Kevin and Scharlotte Fortinberry hosted the 2011 Greene County Fallen Officers Memorial Ceremony.

Mark Green, Jake Green's great-nephew, initiated the process of creating the Mississippi Department of Archives and History (MDAH) historical highway marker and has been a constant supporter.

Carolie Heyliger, my Washington connection and Senior Research Manager for NLEOM.

Sara McGee, the Perry County Historical Society president in 2016, invited me to share my request for information on fallen officers.

The late Janie Adams Hollingshead, Johnny Adams's niece, supplied family history.

Sheriff Victor Mason, sheriff of Hinds County, Mississippi in 2016, assisted with completing paperwork for jailer Russ Harris to be recognized by NLEOM.

The late Police Chief Jerry Gardner with his administrative assistant, Donna Shipley, assisted with filing Dunnam and Millstead's paperwork to the NLEOM.

Officer James Bunch, present Chief of Police for Richton, Mississippi, assisted me with graveside research and local connections in Richton.

Todd Dorsett, whose Find a Grave connection led to finding Judith Wallace.

Judith Wallace, the great-niece of jailer Russ Harris, shared her twenty-page research paper about her great-uncle's death.

Ken Slade, a fellow researcher of the Bond Family, shared several newspaper articles on Henry Bond.

Jim Woodrick, who guided me through the process of obtaining approval for the MDAH historical highway marker.

"Brother" Rogers, MDAH representative at the Centennial Celebration and beyond.

Krista Guice, the Memorial Highway coordinator for the Southeastern District of Mississippi Department of Transportation (MDOT), guided me through the sign dedication process.

Cape Jones, the MDOT engineer who worked to have both memorial signs—from MDAH and MDOT—placed before the Centennial Celebration on April 1, 2021.

Michael Flood, who represented MDOT at the Centennial Ceremony.

Jeff Nowakowski, Public Information Officer for the Southeastern Region of the Bureau of Alcohol, Tobacco, Firearms and Explosives.

Director of the Greene County Museum and Historical Society, the late Alma Douglas, and her administrative assistant, the late Bobbie Pierce, aided me greatly in my search for documents.

Becky Rhinehart, 2024 President of the Greene County Historical Society, for her constant encouragement and support.

The Greene County Board of Supervisors (GCBOS) in 2020 for their assistance and support of memorial highway signage.

Elton Clark, 2021 President of the GCBOS, for his part in the Centennial Celebration.

The late Gary L. Dearman, President of the GCBOS, when I first petitioned the board for the memorial highway signage in 2020.

Mississippi Senator Dennis Debar and Representative Dale Goodin, from 2020-2021, assisted with the passage of the historical signage legislation and several amendments.

Ken Avera, the 2021 Greene County Museum and Historical Society's president, and his late wife, Linda, for their assistance and encouragement while planning and during the Centennial Celebration.

Be Freeman and family for their assistance and financial support of the Centennial Celebration in memory of her grandfather, Lawrence Dunnam.

Brandon Welford who shared his beautiful voice with us at the Centennial Celebration.

MHP Lieutenant Wayne Dearman and the Mississippi Highway Patrol Honor Guard for the presentation of arms at the Centennial Celebration.

First Baptist Church of Sand Hill for their gracious use of facilities for the Centennial Celebration.

Chris Stafford of Stafford Studios created the Centennial Celebration video.

Robert Davis coordinated the placement of Granddaddy Green's name on the Mississippi Fallen Officers Wall in 2021.

Shonna Pierce Designs provided technical support for numerous media challenges and website design.

Russell Turner, Editor of the *Greene County Herald* and *The Richton Dispatch*, for his assistance as I researched the Piney Woods Creek Murders.

My Leakesville Elementary fourth grade and Leakesville Junior High School sixth grade classes encouraged me to write this story I shared with them as part of my Mississippi History curriculum.

Scott, Dan, and Rod—the Woodford Ridge Guys—who graciously allowed Sherye and me the use of their handsome lodge, truly a writer's paradise.

I have been extremely blessed throughout my life with many godly inspirations, but God himself gets full credit for instilling in me, at a young age, His spirit of right and wrong and inwardly encouraging me always to do my best to shine for Him.

My many blessings flow.

Juanita Green Hollinghead
2024

❖ ❖ ❖

As a former history teacher and a student of the same, Juanita's invitation to join her on this adventure has provided me a front-row seat into the details of one of the most riveting criminal cases in Mississippi's history and that of America's Prohibition era. Thank you for including me on this memorable journey.

How incredibly grateful I am to the following individuals for the critical roles they played in assisting me in the polishing of this story:

Juanita's husband, Andy Hollinghead, her son Drew and his wife Elisabeth, and her daughter Paige and her husband Chris, for your many kindnesses to me during my visits to Leakesville.

Juanita's sisters, Debbie Green McLeod and Lisa Green Hedegaard, for your encouragement, hospitality, preparation of many delicious meals, and, most of all, friendship.

Juanita's first cousin, Joy Taylor, for your wise literary advice and for offering a glimpse into your grandmother's life.

My brother, Heber Simmons, III, for your insights and explanations of legal jargon so that I could clearly articulate the proceedings of a 1920s-era courtroom.

The Honorable Randy Pierce, for your inspiring Foreword to this book and your wise counsel regarding many legal aspects of this story.

Stephen Parks, for your assistance with Mississippi criminal statutes from the 1920s.

Eugene H. Stockstill, Jr., for sharing your knowledge of the intricacies of early twentieth-century Mississippi newspaper sources.

Shelley Smith Mitchell, Cedell Hendricks, and Amy Wiandt, for your technical expertise.

Jeff Nowakowski, Public Information Officer with the New Orleans field office of the Bureau of Alcohol, Tobacco, Firearms and Explosives, for your insights into Jake's murder case and your support of this project.

Publisher Lawrence Knorr, Publishing Assistant Katie Cressman, our editors Amanda Krieger and Anaya Montgomery, Book Designer Crystal Devine, Manager of Marketing and Publicity John Jordan, and the talented team at Sunbury Press, for your belief in this story.

Writing is a craft that requires mental and emotional stamina and significant quantities of quiet, uninterrupted time to complete the task. How grateful I am to Dan Dunn, Scott Leininger, Rod Short, and Laura Leathers for your provision of charming, peaceful settings where I could steal away, turn off the world, and write.

My dear friends in the Hallowed Hearts Bible study for your faithful prayers that fueled the discipline and endurance necessary to complete this endeavor.

My husband Mark, from whom I first heard this story all those years ago. Thank you for your unwavering support and confidence in my literary abilities.

My son Mark and daughter-in-law Abigail and my daughter Lauren and son-in-law Clif, for cheering me on during this project.

My parents, Heber and Sister Simmons, and my brother and sister-in-law, Heber and Sperry Simmons, for all your encouragement.

Most of all, thanks to my Lord, who has given me this gift to steward.

Sherye S. Green
2024

A Word from Sherye Green

MY fascination with true-crime stories began early in my life. Always an avid reader, I discovered two books in my junior high and high school days—one about the kidnapping and murder of Charles Lindbergh's infant son and the other about the horrific Hollywood murders of actress Sharon Tate and four others. By the end of the first page of each, I was hooked. In 2010, while in my second career of education, I completed a Master of Social Science in History and Administration of Justice. I taught criminal justice courses at a local community college for several enjoyable years afterward. As I possessed no real-world knowledge and knew my students would need much more than my mastery of the textbook and my fascination with "Law & Order," I enlisted the aid of several seasoned professionals working in law enforcement and in the youth court system, who came on regularly scheduled class visits to share their expertise and street smarts with those in my classes.

Collaborating with Juanita to bring her grandfather's story to life has been especially meaningful for me, as one of Jake's great-nephews, Mark Green, is my husband. Soon after meeting in the fall of 1974, we became high school sweethearts. During the late 1970s, while in college, is my earliest memory of hearing many retellings of this intriguing true-crime case centered around Jake's heroic life and untimely death. Once married and officially becoming a Green, I have had the joy of getting to know

Juanita and her sisters, Debbie and Lisa, and their families. More than cousins by marriage, we are friends.

The experience of coming alongside Juanita has been like traveling through a time capsule. Since she earnestly began to discover the facts of her Granddaddy Green's murder and that of fellow law enforcement official Lawrence Dunnam, Juanita has amassed various primary documents, sources, and artifacts related to the case. As I only joined her while on the last leg of this journey, I've been able to touch the face of a Mississippi historical event that has utterly captivated me.

The most poignant aspect of the story of the Piney Woods Creek Murders is that in addition to the terrible loss of a husband and father, generations of Juanita's family failed to adequately address that grief, as they were never allowed to openly discuss or question the events of that very sorrow-filled spring of 1921. I am proud of Jake's granddaughter for her courage and unwavering spirit to discover the truth at all costs. Jake would be beaming from ear to ear with pride over Juanita's monumental accomplishment. Because of this fearless lady's tireless efforts, many on both sides of the coin, as she likes to say, have made peace with the ghosts of the past and the senseless actions of five men that stole a lifetime of love and laughter from too many.

May this history lesson shed light on the past so that future generations will not repeat these same mistakes.

Chronology: Birth, Death, and Beyond

1861–1865	Civil War
January 4, 1872	John Russell "Russ" Harris born
July 15, 1876	William Lawrence Dunnam born
July 23, 1880	Silas "Sid" Santiel Baggett born
January 3, 1884	Jacob Francis Green born
May 2, 1884	Henry Alexander Bond born
1886	William "Will" R. Morris born
March 29, 1891	Manlious "Mancy" Floyd Kelly born
July 24, 1892	Eliza Ellen Roberts born
1894	John "Johnny" Adams born
January 1, 1900	First portable camera made by George Eastman
January 7, 1903	Ford Motor Company founded by Henry Ford
January 15, 1906	San Francisco earthquake (2,500 killed)
1907	Mississippi passes first Prohibition legislation

1908-1911	Jake serves term as Deputy Sheriff for Greene County, Mississippi
March 1910	Jake and Eliza are introduced at an arranged meeting by a cousin at a church revival in Neely, Mississippi
December 4, 1910	Wedding of Jake to Eliza Ellen Roberts at her home in McLain
January of 1912	Jake Green starts his term as the youngest sheriff in county history at age twenty-eight
January 11, 1912	Birth of Jake's and Eliza' first child and only daughter, Alise Bernell
April 15, 1912	Sinking of the RMS *Titanic*
August 4, 1913	M. L. Batson and Jake Green jointly purchase river and town lots 1, 2, 3, and 4 in Block 10 of Leakesville Platt
February 19, 1914	M.L. Batson deeds to Jake Green property jointly purchased in 1913
1914	Jake builds their "forever home" in Leakesville for Eliza and Bernell
1914–1918	World War I
November 12, 1915	Birth of Jake's and Eliza's second child and first son, Jacob Francis, Jr.
December 31, 1916	Birth of Jake's and Eliza's third child and second son, William Lafayette

January 7, 1918	Mississippi becomes the first state to ratify the Eighteenth Amendment
January 19, 1919	Eighteenth Amendment ratified
August 1919	Jake ran for Sheriff for a second term but was defeated.
September 1919	Jake becomes interested in seeking a federal law enforcement office position as prohibition officer
October 28, 1919	Passage of the National Prohibition Act via a Congressional override of a presidential veto; also known as the Volstead Act
December 4, 1919	Letter from Martin Miller about Gantt and Harrison request
December 12, 1919	Miller and Gantt letters to influence appointment
December 18, 1919	Letter from Gantt stating job compensation: $1500 year/$240 expenses
	Letter from Martin Miller- no news yet
December 20, 1919	Letter to Jake about letter from Gantt to Miller
1920–1933	Prohibition era in United States
1920	Census information: Jacob (35), Eliza (28), Bernell (7), Jacob (5), and William (4)
January 17, 1920	National Prohibition begins; all liquor licenses become null and void; creation of the

	Prohibition Unit within the U.S. Department of the Treasury; operated within the Internal Revenue Service
January 20,1920	Jake is appointed Federal Prohibition Officer for Southern District of the Gulf Department of Mississippi; receives letter of congratulations from Congressman Pat Harrison
March 4, 1921	Warren G. Harding inaugurated as the 29th President of the United States
March 25, 1921	Green is given a detailed map by Sid Baggett as to the specific site of a working still just inside Greene County
April 1, 1921	Green travels to Richton from Hattiesburg; joined by Lawrence Dunnam, Town Marshal of Richton; raid of still on Piney Woods Creek; location on the Greene/ Perry County Line
	End of Watch: Jacob Francis Green—37 years old
	End of Watch: William Lawrence Dunnam—44 years old
	Bodies of Green and Dunnam taken to Dunnam's home; Green's body taken on to Leakesville
	Henry Bond was taken to hospital with gunshot wound
	Johnny Adams, Mancy Kelly, and William Morris arrested for the Piney Woods Creek murders
April 2, 1921	Death Certificates issued for both officers

April 6, 1921	Sid Baggett placed in Hinds County Jail after being arrested in Hattiesburg in connection with supplying map to Agent Green that led him to site
April 25, 1921	*Venire Facias* (jury summons) issued for jurors; May term of court
May 4, 1921	Letter received by Eliza from U.S. Employees Compensation Commissioner Charles Verrell; compensation information
May 9, 1921	Charges filed against Bond, Kelly, Adams, and Morris – Cases 967, 968 & 969
	The four defendants are transferred to Leakesville by Deputy Sheriff Newton James and Sheriff Webb Walley
May 14, 1921	Jury selection begins before noon hour in Case 967
May 16, 1921	Bond motion filed for *severance* (separation) of case; examination of witnesses begins for Mancy Kelly murder trial; Kelly gives notice of an appeal to Mississippi Supreme Court
May 17, 1921	Attorney for Bond asks for a special *venire* (jury) to try case
May 19, 1921	Jury out for short time; Kelly found guilty of murder in the first degree for Case 967: Green Murder and Case 968: Murder of Dunnam
May 20, 1921	Kelly sentenced to hang July 8 for Case 967 and Case 968

May 25, 1921	Jury box exhausted for Bond and Morris cases and special jury pool of eighty to try Bond
May 26, 1921	Kelly signs to appeal his sentence
	Henry bond trial begins for Cases 967: Murder of Jake Green
May 28, 1921	Judge J. D. Fatheree requests extension of May Session to complete Bond's Trial, due to time expiring at midnight
May 30, 1921	Special jury pool of twenty more men requested
	Verdict from jury for Bond/Refused instruction from State/Found guilty
	Special Brief by Judge J.D. Fatheree
	Bond sentenced to hang
May 31, 1921	Both Kelly and Bond moved to Hinds County Jail (location not made public at the time for safekeeping); Morris and Adams to wait for trial until next term in November
June 8, 1921	List of Defense witnesses; request of Bond's lawyer for copy of notes
June 22, 1921	Will Morris released on bond; in jail since April 9
November 24, 1921	Refused Instructions: Will Morris—Case 969; Morris filed for new trial
February 13, 1922	Mississippi Supreme Court affirms Kelly death sentence; Friday, March 24 set for execution by hanging

February 14, 1922	Kelly family requests a temporary reprieve from Governor Russell in order to secure a stay of execution from the State Board of Pardons; new execution date set for April 14
February 21, 1922	U.S. Senator Paul B. Johnson (MS) introduces a bill to pay $1,500 to estates of fallen officers
March 13, 1922	Governor Russell suspends death sentence of Kelly; allows State Pardon Board to vote
Early April of 1922	Adams remains in Forrest County Jail
April 10, 1922	Board of Pardons meets; votes not to commute the sentence of Kelly
April 11, 1922	Kelly notified of hanging on Friday, April 14
April 13, 1922	Two Greene County Deputy Sheriffs transport Kelly from Hinds County Jail to Leakesville; Kelly writes two letters—one to governor and other to fellow Hinds County Jail prisoners
April 14, 1922	Mancy Kelly commits suicide in Greene County Jail (age 31); leaves suicide note stating he is the only one to blame
May 5, 1922	Interview of Kelly's wife in *The Richton Dispatch*; says husband not a bad prisoner
May 8, 1922	Bond's death sentence affirmed by Mississippi Supreme Court
May 23, 1922	Congress votes to provide $1,500 of relief for family of Dunnam

May 27, 1922	State of Mississippi vs. Adams; Johnny Adams acquitted of murder; turned state's evidence
May 30, 1922	Adams pleads guilty for second count of murder of Green: Case 967
May 31, 1922	Adams not given the choice to plea for manslaughter; enters a technical plea of guilty; chooses not to go to trial; receives sentence of life in prison on the District Attorney's recommendation for turning state's evidence in 1921 trials of Kelly and Bond; charge of manufacturing liquor dropped due to life sentence
June of 1922	Mississippi Supreme Court of Appeals hears Bond appeal; upholds lower court decision to death by hanging
June 14, 1922	Governor Russell grants Bond a reprieve in order for Board of Pardons to act on it in July at their quarterly session; execution date delayed until July 21
	Bond's family visits him; they conspire to sneak a pistol to him so he could use it to escape; sister Eliza "Lizzie" Bond Lott volunteers to carry the gun into the jail
June 27, 1922	Henry Bond pending execution for murder
July 7, 1922	Eliza Lott, sister of Henry Bond, smuggles a pistol, hidden in a sack of tomatoes, into the Hinds County jail
July 12, 1922	Pardon Board Secretary Mary Dinkins states that the death sentence commute to life failed; Bond will hang on Friday, July 21

July 14, 1922	Jackson, Mississippi newspaper article about Russ Harris, Hinds County jailer, looking after three doomed death penalty prisoners—Bond, Leavell and McLaurin
July 18, 1922	Bond murders jailer Russ Harris (age 50); attempts escape from Hinds County Jail; Bond dies in the exchange of gunfire (age 50)
	Greene County Sheriff Webb Walley arrives to transport Bond to Leakesville; discovers that Bond has been killed
	Henry Bond's brother, sister-in-law, sister Lizzie, and her daughter Azzie arrested by Sheriff Graham of Covington County; picked up from Collins by Sheriff Lewis Williams; returned to Jackson in connection with Bond's attempted escape that caused Harris's death
July 19, 1922	Charges filed against family members for conspiracy to commit murder of Officer Harris. All but Azzie were placed in Hinds County Jail. She was taken to home of Constable Simmons.
July 21, 1922	Hinds County Grand Jury hears evidence of contributions to Harris's murder by Bond's sisters, Lizzie Bond Lott and Hattie Bond Slade
July 24, 1922	Bond sisters are charged with aiding Bond with his attempted escape and also for supplying the pistol; indicted as accessories to the murder
July 29, 1922	The trial of Will Morris for Case 969 heard in Greene County Circuit Court; receives a three-year penitentiary sentence

November 24, 1922	Both Bond sisters are indicted by the Hinds County Grand Jury
November 29, 1922	Both sisters plead guilty. Lizzie receives a two-year sentence in Parchman Convict Farm in Sunflower County for delivering the pistol to Henry Bond; Hattie sentenced to six months for supplying the pistol
May 20, 1923	Hattie Bond Slade released from prison after serving six months
May 27, 1930	Administration of the Bureau of Prohibition shifts from the Department of the Treasury to U.S. Department of Justice
December 5, 1933	Ratification of the Twenty-First Amendment; official end of Prohibition
1939–1945	World War II
1939	Johnny Adams dies in a fight with fellow inmate at Parchman Farm
July 7, 1943	Polly and Ruth Green marry in North Carolina, where Polly is stationed in the Army awaiting transfer to Germany
1947	Polly elected Sheriff of Greene County
1948	Polly's term as sheriff begins and raids whiskey stills, too
1950	Memorial stained-glass window purchased and installed at Leakesville United Methodist Church

December 15, 1956   Sid Baggett dies

June 26, 1971   Bernell dies in car accident

1978   Eliza Green shows her granddaughter, Lisa, some documents she has kept since Jake was killed

    Eliza enters a long-term care nursing facility due to declining health and vision problems

1979   Eliza's home rented to help generate income for her medical expenses

1980   Steve and Brenda Smith rent Eliza's house

1981–1983   Lisa and Tom Landon rent Eliza's house

January 9, 1984   Andy and Juanita Hollinghead rent Eliza's house

September 3, 1984   Juanita begins her teaching career at Central Elementary School, in George County—second grade

August of 1985   Juanita begins a sixteen-year tenure as fourth-grade teacher at Leakesville Elementary School

    Starts sharing the story of her grandfather getting killed in Greene County in 1921 as part of her Mississippi History curriculum

1986   Andy and Juanita purchase their first house in the Pine Level Community

October 30, 1986   Wiggle dies in automobile accident after suffering an aneurysm

July 30, 1987	Eliza "Mimi" Ellen Roberts Green dies in nursing home at age 96; is buried beside Jake in McLeod-Magnolia Cemetery in Leakesville
November 12, 1987	Lisa Green Landon has her first child, Elizabeth, on Polly's birthday
	Polly, after a lengthy period of health issues, is diagnosed with stomach cancer; treatments begin almost immediately
May of 1988	Polly gives Juanita "The Satchel," containing Polly Wiggle Joy Corporation checkbook and important papers; she will take over his position as treasurer
Late June of 1988	Polly goes into hospital with complications of cancer
July 2, 1988	Polly dies from cancer at Forrest General Hospital, in Hattiesburg, Mississippi; Juanita and Ruth are with him at his death
July 3, 1988	Polly buried in the McLeod-Magnolia Cemetery
March 24, 1989	Jake and Eliza Green family home is sold to Jerry K. and Althea Smith
March of 1991	Andy appointed to the position of Conservation Officer for Greene County with the Mississippi Department of Wildlife, Fisheries and Parks
October of 1991	Without the Green family's knowledge, Jake's name is engraved on the National Law Enforcement Officers Memorial (NLEOM); recognized at the NLEOM's first ceremony

Jake's name is placed on the ATF Fallen Officer's Memorial Wall at the Federal Building in Washington, D.C.; eleventh Fallen Officer as a Special Agent for the ATF

November 7, 1992   Andy and Juanita purchase her parents' home; mother, Ruth, remains and lives with them

Rufus Walley is hired to build bathroom cabinet fronts for Hollinghead home; he apologizes to Juanita for his uncle killing her grandfather

November 19, 1992   Andy is a Game Warden; leads officers on raid of a working whiskey still in Greene County

July 1, 1997   Juanita begins an eight-year tenure on the Board of Alderman for Town of Leakesville

May of 1999   Juanita resigns position as teacher at Leakesville Elementary in order to stay home and care for her mother, Ruth, who has major health issues

2000   Juanita begins researching satchel documents; eyes opened to treasures

Bernell's daughter, Joy plans a visit to catch up with Ruth, as her health is slowly deteriorating

Polly's satchel contents are shared with Joy

Lisa reveals she has a box of papers with historical information from period when Granddaddy Green was killed

October 4, 2002   Ruth Iladean Herring Green dies at Forrest General Hospital after heart attack and multiple health issues

February of 2003	Juanita serves as substitute kindergarten teacher for six weeks at Sand Hill Elementary
June of 2003	Juanita applies for, but is not hired, as principal at Sand Hill Elementary; begins teaching sixth-grade language arts and social studies at Leakesville Junior High and shares the story of Granddaddy Green's death with students
August 4, 2004	Juanita joins BeautiControl as an independent consultant; meets Tiffany Walley Smith (Rufus Walley's granddaughter) at training session; gets Rufus' phone number
November of 2005	Andy and Juanita Hollinghead sell the Leakesville Homeplace to Dorian and Fred Heindl
April of 2006	Juanita begins principalship at Leakesville Elementary School following death of current school district administrator
June of 2006	Andy completes an addition to Hollinghead camp house; family moves to Camp Polly Field
March of 2007	Meeting with Rufus Walley scheduled; Walley dies from complications of surgery before meeting held
May 31, 2007	Juanita resigns as principal at Leakesville Elementary School
August of 2007	Juanita begins job at Sand Hill School as supervisor and instructional interventionist

May 29, 2008	Dedication of new ATF building; Jacob F. Green's name found on ATF Wall of Honor in Washington
May 26, 2011	Fallen Officers of Greene County, Mississippi, Memorial Service for Jake Green and Murdock McIntosh
January 15, 2012	Juanita begins presenting programs of history of Camp Polly Wiggle and Granddaddy Green's death for Junior Miss retreats
February 29, 2012	Juanita retires from Greene County School System; begins work with Discovery Education's Evaluation and Webinar Team
November of 2013	Greene County, Mississippi votes on Wet-Dry Issue; Juanita brokenhearted as wet wins
	Juanita vows to spend time investigating more into Granddaddy's death
April of 2014	Chris Turner, Juanita's son-in-law, introduces her to his step-grandfather, Rayford Freeman; shares his childhood memories of living around Piney Woods Creek
April 3, 2014	Files request to Mississippi Department of Archives and History (MDAH) to research murders; unsuccessful
April 4, 2014	Juanita receives response from U.S. Department of Justice regarding Freedom of Information Act request for information about the murders; unsuccessful

November of 2014	Reunion with Tiffany Walley Smith at Sonlight Community Church service at Greene County High School
January 14, 2015	Google Search of Henry A. Bond reveals ATF listing of Jacob F. Green and Mississippi Supreme Court Cases Argued and Decided
	Historical presentation to Distinguished Young Woman (formally Junior Miss) Retreat at Camp Polly Wiggle; meets Rufus Walley's great niece
January 15, 2015	Juanita visits Rufus Walley's widow, Hazel, with Rufus' friend, David Smith
January 30, 2015	Request made to Cecelia Bounds, Greene County Circuit Clerk, for search of court documents related to the 1921 case
January 31, 2015	Text received from Clerk Bounds; info found
	Three court document folders located: Case 967 - Bond, Case 967 – Adams, and Case 969 - Morris
	Online search results reveal Kelly v State No 22047
February 2, 2015	Juanita visits Greene County Museum; discovers "My Mayberry Museum"
February 3, 2015	Online investigation of Henry Bond; discovery of ATF site linked to appeal to Mississippi Supreme Court
February 9, 2015	Juanita visits Richton Police Department; visits Sunset Cemetery; takes pictures of all Dunnam headstones

	Visits *The Richton Dispatch* newspaper office
	Visits the University of Southern Mississippi Library
February 27, 2015	Juanita attempts to notify ATF to try to gain any information on case; no results
March 5, 2015	Juanita locates NLEOM Officer Down Memorial Page/ Line 12 #4 Row 12, Panel 1, Jacob F Green, W16: 12
May 12, 2015	Juanita meets Diane Goodnight, Mancy Kelly's great niece; hears stories of her Uncle Mancy and his suicide
	Visits Frisco Cemetery and photographs graves of persons named Adams; finds one with name of Johnny Adams on it
May 16, 2015	Sarah Magee, President of Perry County Historical Society, asks Juanita to come speak of her request for any connections to the 1921 murders and connected with Janie Adams Hollingshead (Johnny Adams's niece)
May 24, 2015	Juanita substitutes at Greene County High School for Paula Hensley; greeted by Prohibition teaching unit on her planning desk
June 2015	Juanita requests a death certificate for Jacob F. Green as his grandchild
August 6, 2015	Juanita joins Greene County Historical Society and starts volunteering at Greene County Museum

August 19, 2015   Google search: Southern Reporter, Kelly v State
                   Volume 90

                   Bond v State Volume 91

January 2016   Juanita discovers the obituary of Lawrence
                   Dunnam's youngest child, Willye Dunnam
                   McLain; notes two sons as survivors: Mike and
                   Morgan, Jr.

February 2, 2016   Juanita discovers cassette tape of recording of
                   Mimi's (Eliza's) interview by her brother, Jake;
                   Eliza recalls on the tape how she and Jake met

February 14, 2016 Juanita pays Spokeo $1.95 for search of McLain
                   survivors' contact information

                   Juanita contacted Lawrence Dunnam's youngest
                   grandson, Morgan McLain, through Spokeo
                   information site, and schedules a visit at his
                   home in Mobile

February 16, 2016 Juanita meets with Morgan and Bessie McLain
                   to gain any information

Late February 2016 Works with Richton Police Chief Jerry Gardner
                   and his secretary, Donna Shipley, and with
                   Hinds County Sheriff Mason and his secretary
                   to complete NLEOM applications for Dunnam,
                   Milstead, and Harris

                   Find a Grave comment request led to con-
                   nection to Jailer Harris's Family: contacted
                   his great niece, Judith Wallace, who sent to
                   Juanita a twenty-page research paper that she

wrote in 1984 for an education class: "A Tale of Tragedy:1922 Shootout at the Old Jackson Jail"

March 7, 2016   Juanita contacts David Smith, previous owner of murder site property to request contact info for present owner, Kevin Nicholson; Nicholson agrees to allow Green family members to visit the property on the ninety-fifth anniversary of Jake's death: April 1, 2016

March 18, 2016   Juanita receives letter from ATF in response to request for information on Green

Juanita receives two free hours of research search time on gaining knowledge of his file; Disclosure Division calls Juanita to inform her that Jake's file was destroyed in the 1950's in a fire. However, the ATF has honored him every year at the NLEOM Wall

March 30, 2016   Juanita calls Kevin Nicholson to postpone visit due to prediction of bad weather; is invited to visit murder site that day; Juanita immediately drives to site and requests another visit on April 1

April 1, 2016   Green family members join Juanita at property site; tour still property; *Greene County Herald* article about visit

May 14, 2016   Juanita sends message to Harris Family through SPOKEO and Find a Grave search results to try to connect with family of jailer who was killed

July 15, 2016   Successful Find a Grave search uncovered Bond Family burial plots but no Henry A. Bond:

Hester(mother), Henry L.(father) John, Isaac, and Jack Bond—all in Lamar County, MS

July 21, 2016 — Juanita calls Parchman Prison to try and gain information on inmates Morris, Adams, Baggett, Slade, and Lott; sends Superintendent Ernest Lee an email request for information; referred to Jasmine Cole in Jackson; Cole returns Juanita's request stating she did not have any of that information

July 26, 2016 — Juanita works to gain information about Henry Bond's gravesite; researches his granddaughter, Voncile Smith; finds out Henry's wife had lived with Voncile until her death; buried in Clark County

October 7, 2016 — Juanita receives NLEOM Confirmation Notification from Carolie Heyliger; NLEOM approves Dunnam's and Millstead's names for the memorial wall

October 29, 2016 — Juanita receives two official letters from the NLEOM: confirmation of Dunnam and Millstead being approved for 2017 addition and request for names of survivors for invitations to the ceremony in May 2017

November 16, 2016 — Todd Dorsett, Juanita's connection to the Russ Harris Family, emails picture of the Hinds County jailer

February 2017 — Juanita receives confirmation that Harris will be another addition to the NLEOM wall in May

May of 2017	Juanita attends NLEOM Candlelight Vigil during Police Week activities in Washington, D. C.; accompanied by her sister, Debbie Green McLeod, and Debbie's son, Benji, and daughter-in-law Mollie
	Visits memorial wall in Jackson where the three newest of Juanita's Mississippi Men are added; Jake's name not on wall; Juanita decides to investigate
April 1, 2020	Juanita sends request to Greene County Board of Supervisors for Memorial Highway Sign proposal and support of MDAH Historical Marker
April 6, 2020	Juanita attends Greene County Board of Supervisor's meeting; two-fold proposal on agenda: to have highway section renamed and submit historical marker application; both voted on and approved; sent to legislature
October 2020	Juanita contacts Robert Davis (Mississippi Sheriff's Association) about omission of Green's name on Mississippi Fallen Officers Memorial (MFOM) wall in Jackson; sends him proof of NLEOM marker; Davis approves addition of names in April of 2021
April 1, 2021	Signage ceremony for MDAH and MDOT signs to be dedicated:
	Memorial Highway Sign and Historical Marker; almost one hundred guests attend private ceremony at First Baptist Church of Sand Hill

April 13, 2021   Juanita receives email from Robert Davis
                      with pictures showing that Green's name has
                      been added to the Mississippi Fallen Officer's
                      Memorial Wall; included on April 12, 2021

April 14, 2021   Robert Davis email states Police Chief's
                      Association will sponsor the Candlelight
                      Ceremony at 6:30 P.M. on May 11

May 11, 2021   Candlelight Vigil postponed due to weather
                      until May 18 at 6 P.M.

May 18, 2021   Andy and Juanita visit the Two Mississippi
                      Museums in Jackson; tour special Prohibition
                      Exhibit

                      Attend the 2021 Mississippi Fallen Officers
                      Candlelight Vigil for Fallen Officers at Fallen
                      Officers Memorial Wall, Jackson, Mississippi

The Cast of Characters

THE VICTIMS AND THEIR FAMILIES

Jacob Francis Green
- Greene County, Mississippi Sheriff 1912–1915.
- US Deputy Marshall as a Prohibition Officer serving the Gulf Department of the U.S. Treasury Department 1920–1921.
- End of Watch (EOW): April 1, 1921 Raiding a Whiskey Still in Greene County.

Eliza Ellen Roberts Green
- Wife of Jacob Francis Green, Sr.
- Housewife and mother of three: Alise Bernell, Jacob Francis, Jr., and William Lafayette.

William Lawrence Dunnam
- Town Marshal for Richton, Mississippi 1921.
- Greene County, Mississippi Deputy Sheriff 1921.
- EOW: April 1, 1921 raiding a Whiskey Still in Greene County.

THE MOONSHINERS AND THEIR FAMILIES

Johnny M. Adams
- Convicted of the murder of Lawrence Dunam and Jake Green Case 967 in 1921 at 27 years of age.
- He turned against his fellow moonshiners and pled guilty. Turned state's evidence and was given life in prison instead of the hanging gallows.
- Died in Parchman Prison in 1939 from wounds suffered in a fight with another inmate at age forty-five.

217

Sid Baggett

- Resident of Sumrall, Mississippi. Bootlegger in his neck of the woods and competitor of Henry Bond in shiny business.
- Drew a map that would lead one to the whiskey still that Bond was overseeing in Perry County. Was also thought to have alerted the moonshiners that the officers were coming.
- Arrested on April 5 in Greene County, Mississippi, and taken to Hinds County (Mississippi) jail. Served time at Parchman Prison for his contribution to the murders of Green and Dunnam.

Henry Alexander Bond

- Perry County, Mississippi resident originally from Lamar County, Mississippi.
- Convicted of murder of Lawrence Dunam and Jake Green Case 967 in 1921.
- Appealed case and sent to Hinds County, Mississippi jail for safe-keeping for part of 1921 and 1922.
- Lost his appeal.
- The day he was to be picked up and taken to Greene County to be hanged, Bond attempted escape by using a gun that was slipped to him by his sister in a prior visit.
- He shot Jailer Russ Harris, and Harris shot him.
- Both Bond and Harris died that day in July 1922.

Hester Cameron Bond

- Henry Bond's mother.

Isaac Bond

- Henry Bond's brother; married to Nancy Bond.

Ellen Bond

- Henry Bond's wife.

Manlious "Mancy" Floyd Kelly

- Perry County, Mississippi resident.
- Convicted of murder of Lawrence Dunam and Jake Green Case 967 in 1921.
- Appealed case and sent to Hinds County, Mississippi jail for safe-keeping 1921–1922.

- Taken to Greene County to be hanged after the appeal was denied.
- Slit his throat minutes from being taken to the gallows in July of 1922.
- Wife, Lydia, and children Virgil (10), Hurthia (8), and Lois (4) witnessed his suicide.

Eliza "Lizzie" Bond Lott
- Henry Bond's sister smuggled her sister Hattie's pistol into the Hinds County jail hidden in a sack of tomatoes.
- Was convicted and served time in Parchman Penitentiary.

Will Morris
- He had participated in the manufacturing of the whiskey at Bond's Still, and although he was at the still on April 1, 1921, he did not participate in the gunfight that killed the officers.
- Case 969: convicted of manufacturing and distribution of intoxicating liquor and served 3 years at Parchman Prison. He made several attempts to have his sentence shortened.

Hattie Bond Slade
- Henry Bond's sister who supplied the gun with which Henry shot and killed jailer Russ Harris.

Azzie Bond
- Daughter of Henry Bond; twelve years old at time of his death.

HELPFUL CITIZENS

Dr. R. M. Cochran of Richton
- Called to the home of Henry Bond on April 1, 1921, to administer assistance for Bond's gunshot wound. He had no idea that Bond was involved in murders at the time. Had Bond sent to Laurel Hospital with wounds that appeared to be fatal.

Mr. Rogers
- Resident of McLain, Mississippi.
- Taxi driver for the Richton area in 1921.
- Drove Green and Dunnam to the drop off sight from where they approached the still.

- If they did not return, he was to call for assistance.
- Phoned authorities to tell them he heard gunshots and that something might have happened to Green and Dunnam.

Reverend F. W. Johnson
- Methodist minister called upon to visit Mancy Kelly in jail in the hours before his execution was to take place on Friday, April 14, 1922.
- Witnessed Kelly's suicide.

MISSISSIPPI LAW ENFORCEMENT OFFICERS

Constable O.E. Carter
- Worked in Hattiesburg, Mississippi and Perry County, Mississippi in 1921.
- Will Morris confessed his part in the murders to him.

Sheriff Dennis
- Sheriff of Perry County, Mississippi in 1921.
- Interviewed Henry Bond in the hospital in Laurel on night of or day after murders.

Sheriff Graham
- Sheriff of Covington County, Mississippi in 1921.

John Russell "Russ" Harris
- Deputy Sheriff and Jailer for Hinds County, Mississippi in Raymond in 1921-22.
- Fatally shot by Henry Bond as Bond was attempting escape but not before Harris returned the fatal shot to Bond.

Henry Heveron
- Jailer at Hinds County jail in Jackson, Mississippi.
- Was to have been on duty while fellow jailer Russ Harris was away on a fishing trip.

O.W. Ladner
- Deputy Sheriff for Lamar County, Mississippi.

Frank McKensie
- Jailer in Forrest County.

- Locked up Morris, Kelly, and Adams in the Hattiesburg jail.
- Served as a witness for Adams during his trial.

W. D. Mills
- Justice of the Peace for Richton.
- Accompanied Henry Bond to the Laurel Hospital from gunshot to chest area.

Benjamin Manuel "B. M." Millstead
- Former town marshal of Richton.
- Murdered at age forty-four on April 17, 1920.

Sheriff E. D. Edmonson
- Sheriff of Forest County, Mississippi in 1921.
- Transferred Kelly, Morris, and Adams to Jackson from jail in Hattiesburg.

Jonathan Turner
- Deputy Sheriff of Greene County, Mississippi in Leakesville.
- Witnessed Mancy Kelly's suicide in 1922.

Sheriff Webb Walley
- Greene County Mississippi's Sheriff in 1916–1923.

Sheriff Lewis Williams
- Sheriff of Hinds County, Mississippi, at time of the Bond-Harris murders.

MISSISSIPPI GOVERNMENT OFFICIALS

Mayor J. T. Allums
- Mayor of Richton, Mississippi in 1921.

Governor Lee M. Russell
- 40th Governor of the State of Mississippi.
- Term of office: January 18, 1920 – January 18, 1924.

PROHIBITION AGENTS AND OFFICERS

J. L. Boyd
- Prohibition agent working in Jackson under direction of Ellis Chapman.

J. L. Buchanan
- Prohibition agent working in Newton, Mississippi.

Ellis S. Chapman
- Supervising federal Prohibition agent of Mississippi.
- Arrived at the murder scene the morning of Saturday, April 2.

D. J. Gantt, Esq.
- Supervising Federal Prohibition Agent; Atlanta, Georgia.

Deputy U.S. Marshal W. L. Eshi
- Prohibition agent in Meridian, MS.

U.S. Marshal Floyd Loper
- In charge of the Southern District of Mississippi for U.S. Marshals Service.

Deputy U.S. Marshal A.W. Loposser
- Prohibition agent stationed in Biloxi, Mississippi, for U.S. Marshals Service.

Deputy U.S. Marshal Cuyler Thames
- Prohibition officer in Mendenhall, Mississippi, for U.S. Marshals Service.

Deputy U.S. Marshal A. W. Thompson
- Prohibition officer in Dekalb, Mississippi.

Major Calvin Wells
- Federal Director of Prohibition Enforcement in Mississippi.

Deputy U.S. Marshal Glenn O. Whitehead
- Prohibition agent working under the direction of Ellis Chapman.

TRIAL JUDGES

The Honorable J.D. Fatheree
- Judge for the court cases in Greene County 1921-1923.

The Honorable Oscar Flowers
- Presided over a court case against Henry Bond's sisters, Lizzie Bond Lott and Hattie Bond Slade.

COUNSEL FOR THE PROSECUTION

E. W. Breland
- Attorney from Leakesville, Mississippi.
- Represented the State of Mississippi in the Mancy Kelly trial.

E.C. Fishel
- Represented the State of Mississippi in the Mancy Kelly trial.

Hugh Gillespie
- Attorney in Jackson, Mississippi.
- Prosecutor in the trials of Henry Bond's sisters, Eliza Bond Lott and Hattie Bond Slade.

Charles B. Hamilton
- Assistant Prosecutor in the trials of Henry Bond's sisters, Eliza Bond Lott and Hattie Bond Slade.

H. Cassidy Holden
- Special assistant with the Mississippi Attorney General's office.
- Represented the State of Mississippi in the case of Mancy Kelly's appeal to the Mississippi Supreme Court.

J. W. Howie
- District Attorney of Hinds County, Mississippi.
- Represented the State of Mississippi in the trials of Henry Bond's sisters, Eliza Bond Lott and Hattie Bond Slade.

Martin V. B. Miller
- District Attorney for the Tenth District; Meridian, Mississippi.
- Assisted Jake in gaining the position as prohibition officer.
- Assisted in the investigation and prosecution of all involved in the murders.

John Robert Tally
- Lawyer for the State at murder trials.

COUNSEL FOR THE DEFENSE

Cephus Anderson
- Attorney from Hattiesburg, Mississippi.

- Represented Henry Bond at his murder trial.
- Son and law partner of Elisha Alexander "Zan" Anderson.

Elisha Alexander "Zan" Anderson
- Attorney from Hattiesburg, Mississippi.
- Represented Henry Bond at his murder trial.
- Father and law partner of Cephus Anderson.
- Former member of the Mississippi House of Representatives.

Elmer Busby
- Attorney from Waynesboro, Mississippi.
- Represented Mancy Kelly at his murder trial.

Marian W. Reilly
- Attorney from Meridian, Mississippi.
- Represented Mancy Kelly at his murder trial.

Bibliography

Blumenthal, Karen. *Bootleg: Murder, Moonshine, and the Lawless Years of Prohibition.* New York: Flash Point, 2011.

Dison, Brad. *Whiskey and Blood.* Saline: Harper Hill Publishing, 2017.

Harris, Wesley. *Neither Fear Nor Favor: Deputy United States Marshal John Tom Sisemore.* Ruston: RoughEdge Publications, 2017.

Horning, Chuck and B. Lee Charlton. *Trail of Shadows: The Unsolved Murders of Prohibition Agents Dale Kearney and Ray Sutton.* Jefferson: McFarland & Company, Inc., Publishers, 2019.

Ray, T.J. *Side by Side: Moonshine and Murder in Mississippi.* Gretna: Pelican Publishing Company, Inc., 2016.

Tracy, Janice Branch. *Mississippi Moonshine Politics: How Bootleggers & the Law Keep a Dry State Soaked.* Charleston: The History Press, 2015.

Notes

CHAPTER ONE: JAKE GREEN'S FAMILY WEB

1. Daryn Glassbrook, "The History of Yellow Fever in Mobile," *Mobile Bay*, July 28, 2021, accessed July 14, 2022, https://mobilebaymag.com/the-history-of -yellow-fever-in-mobile/.

2. "Notes from McLain: The Greene-Roberts Wedding," *Greene County Herald* (Leakesville, Mississippi), December 5, 1910.

CHAPTER TWO: "THE WETTEST DRY STATE"

1. Jere Nash, "Edmund Favor Noel (1908-1912) and the Rise of James K. Vardaman and Theodore G. Bilbo," *The Journal of Mississippi History* Volume LXXXI, no. 1 and no. 2 (Spring/Summer 2019), https://www.mississippihistory.org/sites/default/diles/ spring_summer_2019_final.pdf.

2. Ann Marie Cunningham, "Mississippi: Legally Dry but Soaking Wet and Often Violent," *Mississippi Center for Investigative Reporting*, November 10, 2020, accessed March 25, 2023, https://www.mississippicir.org/perspective/mississippi -legally-dry-but-soaking-wet-and-often-violent.

3. *Britannica Online Encyclopedia*, s.v. "Volstead Act," accessed March 22, 2023, https://www.britannica.com/print/article/632412.

4. Ibid.

5. "Twenty-First Amendment," *Constitution Annotated*, accessed March 22, 2023, https://constitution.congress.gov/constitution/amendment-21/.

6. "Reorganization of Prohibition Enforcement," *CQ Researcher*, accessed May 30, 2023, https://library.cqpress.com/cqresearcher/document.php?id=cqresrre 1929090200.

7. "Prohibition Agents Lacked Training, Numbers to Battle Bootleggers," *The Mob Museum*, accessed April 7, 2023, https://prohibition_themobmuseum.org/the-history/ enforcing-the-prohibition-laws/law-enforcement-during-prohibition/.

8. Ibid.

9. "U.S. Marshals Role During Prohibition," *U.S. Marshals Service*, accessed March 5, 2023, https://www.usmarshals.gov/who-we-are/about-us/history/historical -reading-room/us-marshals-role-during-prohibition.

10. Ibid.

11. Regina Lombardo to Juanita Hollinghead, April 1, 2021.

12. "Prohibition," *Mississippi Encyclopedia*, Ted Ownby, University of Mississippi, accessed March 5, 2023, https://mississippiencyclopedia.org/entries/prohibition.

13. Leah Willingham, "90 Years Later, Prohibition officially ending in Mississippi," *The Washington Post*, July 2, 2020, accessed August 24, 2022, https://www.washingtonpost.com/business/90-years-later-prohibition-officially-ending-in-mississippi/2020/07/02/19f02478-bcb0-11ea-97c1-6cf116ffe26c_story.html.

14. Ibid.

15. Richard Norquist, "Soggy Sweat's Famous Whiskey Speech How to Flatter an Audience with Euphemisms, Dysphemisms, and Distinctio," ThoughtCo, updated on March 11, 2018, accessed March 27, 2023, https://www.thoughtco.com/flatter-an-audience-with-euphemisms-1691833.

16. Ibid.

17. Richard Norquist, "Soggy Sweat's Famous Whiskey Speech How to Flatter an Audience with Euphemisms, Dysphemisms, and Distinctio."

18. Warren Kulo, "Greene County passes referendum to 'go wet,'; voters OK sale of beer, light wine," GulfLive.com, November 27, 2012, accessed August 24, 2022, https://www.gulflive.com/mississippi-press-news/2012/11/greene_county_passes_referendu.html#:~:text=OCEAN%20SPRINGS%2C%20Mississippi%20%2D%2D%20After,of%20beer%20and%20light%20wine.

CHAPTER THREE: JAKE'S CAREER: LOCAL TO FEDERAL

1. Martin V. B. Miller to D. J. Gantt, December 12, 1919.
2. D. J. Gantt to Martin V. B. Miller, December 18, 1919.
3. Martin V. B. Miller to D. J. Gantt, December 20, 1919.

CHAPTER FOUR: THE PINEY WOODS CREEK MURDER

1. Jake Green to Eliza Green, March 31, 1921.

CHAPTER FIVE: THE MANHUNT

1. "Double Tragedy Marks Still Raid," *Greene County Herald* (Leakesville, Mississippi), April 8, 1921.

2. "Confession Made by Will Morris Involves Others: Alleged Slayers of Richton Marshal and Federal Officer Being Closely Guarded," *The Mobile Register* (Mobile, Alabama), April 2, 1921.

3. Ibid.

4. "Two Raiders Die in Battle with Moonshine Band: One Alleged Distiller Shot, Another Jailed in Mississippi," *The Times-Picayune* (New Orleans, Louisiana), April 2, 1921.

5. "Confession Made by Will Morris Involves Others," *The Mobile Register*.

6. "Two Raiders Die in Battle with Moonshine Band: One Alleged Distiller Shot, Another Jailed in Mississippi," *The Times-Picayune*.

7. "Confession Made by Will Morris Involves Others," *The Mobile Register*.

8. Ibid.

9. Ibid.

10. Ibid.

11. Ibid.

12. "Officers Raiding Mississippi Still Are Both Slain," *The Mobile Register* (Mobile,Alabama), April 2, 1921.

13. "Two Officers Killed While Raiding Still," *The Richton Dispatch* (Richton, Mississippi), April 8, 1921.

14. "Mob Mutterings Sends Prisoners to Jackson Jail," *The Daily Herald* (Biloxi, Mississippi), April 6, 1921.

15. "Two Raiders Die in Battle With Moonshine Band."

CHAPTER SIX: LAID TO REST

1. "Officers Here Deplore Death of Officers Near Richton During Raid Friday," *The Gulfport Daily Herald* (Gulfport, Mississippi), April 2, 1921.

2. Ibid.

3. "Two Officers Killed While Raiding Still," *The Richton Dispatch* (Richton, Mississippi), April 8, 1921.

4. "Double Tragedy Mark Still Raid," *Greene County Herald* (Leakesville, Mississippi), April 8, 1921.

5. "Two Officers Killed While Raiding Still," *The Richton Dispatch*.

6. Ibid.

7. "In Memoriam" *The Richton Dispatch* (Richton, Mississippi), date unknown.

8. M. L. Batson, M.D., to Eliza Green, date unknown.

CHAPTER SEVEN: BIRTH OF THE GREEN WIDOW

1. Acting Chairman of United States Employees' Compensation Commission to Eliza Green, May 4, 1921.

2. Ibid.

3. Ibid.

4. Ellis S. Chapman to Eliza Green, July 12, 1921.

5. Ibid.

CHAPTER EIGHT: THE INVESTIGATION

1. "Double Tragedy Marks Still Raid," *Greene County Herald* (Leakesville, Mississippi), April 8, 1921.

2. National Archives Education Team, "Prohibition Enforcement Map Analysis," *Docs Teach*, accessed March 14, 2023, https://docsteach.org/activities/teacher/prohitibition-enforement-map-analysis.

3. Ibid.

4. "Confession Made by Will Morris Involves Others: Alleged Slayers of Richton Marshal and Federal Officer Being Closely Guarded," *The Mobile Register* (Mobile, Alabama), April 2, 1921.

5. "Two Officers Killed While Raiding Still," *The Richton Dispatch* (Richton, Mississippi), April 8, 1921.

6. Ibid.

7. "Four Held in Murder of Two Dry Officers in Richton, Miss.," *New Orleans Item* (New Orleans, Louisiana), April 2, 1921.

8. "Two Officers Killed While Raiding Still."

9. Ibid.

10. "Confession Made by Will Morris Involves Others," *The Mobile Register.*

11. "Two Officers Killed While Raiding Still."

12. Ibid.

13. Ibid.

14. "Double Tragedy Marks Still Raid," *Greene County Herald.*

15. "Two Officers Killed While Raiding Still."

16. "Confession Made by Will Morris Involves Others: Alleged Slayers of Richton Marshal and Federal Officer Being Closely Guarded," *The Mobile Register* (Mobile, Alabama), April 2, 1921.

17. "Mob Mutterings Sends Prisoners to Jackson Jail," *The Daily Herald* (Biloxi, Mississippi), April 6, 1921.

18. Parks, Stephen. Interview by Sherye S. Green. Written answers to questions received by e-mail. May 31, 2023.

19. William Hemingway, *Annotated Mississippi Code Showing the General Statutes in Force* (Indianapolis: The Bobbs-Merrill Company, 1917), p. 702.

20. "Arrested in Double Murder," *The Evening Star* (Washington, D.C.), April 6, 1921.

CHAPTER NINE: PRE-TRIAL MOTIONS

1. *Merriam-Webster*, s.v. "venire facias," accessed March 29, 2023, https://www.merriam-webster.com/dictionary/venirefacias.

2. "The State of Mississippi vs. Mancey F. Kelly, Henry A. Bond, John Adams and Will Morris," Circuit Court, Greene County, Mississippi, May Term 1921.

3. Greene County Circuit Court General Docket, Leakesville, Mississippi, May 9, 1921.

4. Indictment, Circuit Court, Greene County, May Term, 1921, "The State of Mississippi vs. Will Morris, Mancey F. Kelley, Henry A. Bond and John Adams."

5. "Glossary of Legal Terms," s.v. "Capias – Instanter," *State Attorney 18th Judicial District*, accessed March 28, 2023, https://sa18.org/page/legal-terms.html#1's.

6. "Instanter Capias," John W. Colbert, Circuit Clerk, Greene County Circuit Court, Leakesville, Mississippi, May 9, 1921.

7. "Mancy Kelly Convicted," *Greene County Herald* (Leakesville, Mississippi), May 27, 1921.

8. Ibid.

9. "Special Venire for Moonshine Murders," *Laurel Daily Leader* (Laurel, Mississippi), May 20, 1921.

10. "History of the Death Penalty," State and Federal Info Mississippi, *Death Penalty Information Center*, accessed March 3, 2022, https://deathpenaltyinfo.org/state-and-federal-info/state-by-state/mississippi.

11. Ibid.

12. "Richton Moonshine Murderers on Trial," *Laurel Daily Leader* (Laurel, Mississippi), May 11, 1921.

13. *Merriam-Webster*, s.v. "venire," accessed March 29, 2023, https://www.merriam-webster.com/dictionary/venire.

14. "Special Venire for Moonshine Murders," *Laurel Daily Leader*.

15. Final report of the Grand Jury for the May 1921 term, Greene County Circuit Court, Leakesville, Mississippi.

CHAPTER TEN: THE ROPE'S TOO BIG

1. "Circuit Court May Term 1921," *Greene County Herald* (Leakesville, Mississippi), May 27, 1921.

2. "Mancy Kelly Convicted," *Greene County Herald* (Leakesville, Mississippi), May 27, 1921.

3. *Legal Information Institute*, s.v. "voir dire," Cornell Law School, accessed April 5, 2023, https://www.law.cornell.edu/wex/voir_dire.

4. "Circuit Court May Term 1921," *Greene County Herald*.

5. Ibid.

6. Ibid.

7. Ibid.

8. "Officers Raiding Mississippi Still are Both Slain," *The Mobile Register* (Mobile, Alabama), April 2, 1921.

9. "Circuit Court May Term 1921."

10. Ibid.

11. "Special Venire for Moonshine Murderers," *Laurel Daily Leader* (Laurel, Mississippi), May 20, 1921.

12. Handwritten note from jury foreman.

13. "Circuit Court May Term 1921."

14. "To Hang for Killing Dry Officer," *The Richmond Times* (Richmond, Virginia), May 28, 1921.

15. "Governor Suspends Sentence of Kelly," *The Richton Dispatch* (Richton, Mississippi), April 1922.

16. "Kelly to Die, Pardon Board Has Decided," *The Hattiesburg American* (Hattiesburg, Mississippi), April 10, 1922.

17. Ibid.

18. "Mancy F. Kelly Cheats Gallows by Killing Self," *The Richton Dispatch* (Richton, Mississippi), April 21, 1922.

19. "Statement of Jonathan Turner," *Greene County Herald* (Leakesville, Mississippi), date unknown.

20. Ibid.

21. Ibid.
22. Ibid.
23. Ibid.
24. Ibid.
25. Ibid.
26. Ibid.
27. Ibid.
28. Ibid.
29. Ibid.
30. Ibid.
31. Ibid.
32. Ibid.
33. Ibid.
34. Ibid.
35. Ibid.
36. Ibid.
37. Ibid.
38. "Kelly Writes Letter to Governor Russell," *The Richton Dispatch* (Richton, Mississippi), April 21, 1922.
39. "Statement of Jonathan Turner."

CHAPTER ELEVEN: CHEATING THE GALLOWS

1. "Brother of Bond Faces New Trial," *Gulfport Daily News* (Gulfport, Mississippi), July 24, 1922.
2. "KA Bond in the 1920 United States Federal Census," Ancestry.com, accessed May 22, 2015, http://search.ancestry.com/search/collections/1920usfedcen/54121330/printer-friendly.
3. "State vs. Ernest Bond," The State of Mississippi, Greene County Circuit Court, No. 961, Action for being drunk on public road.
4. Indictment of Ernest Bond and John Adams," The State of Mississippi, Greene County Circuit Court, November Term 1920.
5. "Confession made by Will Morris Involves Others: Alleged Slayers of Richton Marshal and Federal Officer Being Closely Guarded," *The Mobile Register* (Mobile, Alabama), April 2, 1921.
6. "M. 180—Special Venire Facias When Jury Box Cannot Be Used," Greene County Circuit Court, Leakesville, Mississippi, May 25, 1921.
7. Working notes of Juanita Green Hollinghead.
8. Ibid.
9. "The State of Mississippi, County of Greene, Circuit Court, May Term, 1921," J.D. Fatheree, Judge 10th Judicial District of the State of Mississippi.
10. "Circuit Court May Term 1921," *The Greene County Herald* (Leakesville, Mississippi), May 27, 1921.
11. "State of Mississippi vs. Henry A. Bond," State of Mississippi, Greene County, Circuit Court, May Term 1921, Case 967.

12. "State of Mississippi vs. Henry A. Bond," Motion to quash the jury, State of Mississippi, Greene County, Circuit Court, May 28, 1921.

13. "Double Tragedy Marks Still Raid, *Greene County Herald* (Leakesville, Mississippi), April 8, 1921.

14. "State of Mississippi vs. Henry A. Bond," Motion to quash the jury.

15. Statement to Counsel from Judge J. D. Fatheree.

16. "Supreme Court Decides Henry Bond Must Hang," *The Hattiesburg American* (Hattiesburg, Mississippi), May 8, 1922.

17. "Bond Doomed by Supreme Court: Must Forfeit Life for the Murder of Prohibition Officers Green and Dunnam in Green County," *The Daily Herald* (Biloxi, Mississippi), May 9, 1922.

18. "Supreme Court Decides Henry Bond Must Hang," *The Hattiesburg American*.

19. Judith Harris Wallace, "A Tale of Tragedy: 1922 Shoot-Out At The Old Jackson Jail" (unpublished manuscript, July 23, 1984), typescript.

20. "Execution of Bond Delayed by Governor," *The Richton Dispatch* (Richton, Mississippi), Jun 16, 1922.

21. "Bond to Hang Friday, July 21st," *The Richton Dispatch* (Richton, Mississippi), July 14, 1922.

22. "Women Confess Part in Murder," *The Times-Picayune* (New Orleans, Louisiana), July 21, 1922.

23. "Bond Kept Gun Hidden in Cell Several Weeks," *The Times-Picayune* (New Orleans, Louisiana), July 24, 1922.

24. "Hinds County Jailer Assassinated in Endeavor to Liberate Henry Bond," *The Daily Herald* (Biloxi, Mississippi), July 19, 1922.

25. "Jailer and Condemned Murderer Fatally Wounded in Pistol Duel: Official, Dying Locks Prison Doors," *The Lexington Herald* (Lexington, Kentucky), July 19, 1922.

26. "Henry Bond Killed By Jailer Whom He Fatally Shot," *Greene County Herald* (Leakesville, Mississippi), July 21, 1922.

27. "Jailer and Condemned Murderer Fatally Wounded in Pistol Duel: Official, Dying Locks Prison Doors," *The Lexington Herald*.

28. "Henry Bond Killed By Jailer Whom He Fatally Shot," *Greene County Herald*.

29. "Jailer and Condemned Murderer Fatally Wounded in Pistol Duel."

30. Ibid.

31. Ibid.

32. Ibid.

33. "Hinds County Jailer Assassinated in Endeavor to Liberate Henry Bond," *The Daily Herald*.

34. Ibid.

35. "Sisters of Bond Are Indicted for Planning Escape—Supreme Court Criminal Docket is Set for November 27th," *The Hattiesburg American* (Hattiesburg, Mississippi), November 24, 1922.

36. Ibid.

37. Ibid.

CHAPTER TWELVE: COHORTS IN CRIME

1. "Circuit Court May Term 1921," Greene County Herald (Leakesville, Mississippi), May 27, 1921.

2. Appearance Bond for Will Morris, The State of Mississippi, Greene County, November 14, 1921.

3. "Indictment: The State of Mississippi vs. Will Morris, Mancey F. Kelley, Henry A. Bond, John Adams, No. 969," Circuit Court, Greene County, Mississippi, May Term 1921.

4. "State vs. Will Morris, No. 969, Motion and Affidavit for Change of Venue," State of Mississippi, Greene County, In Circuit Court, November term, 1921.

5. "Four Held in Murder of Two Dry Officers in Richton, Miss.," *New Orleans Item* (New Orleans, Louisiana), April 2, 1921.

6. "Confession Made by Will Morris Involves Others: Alleged Slayers of Richton Marshal and Federal Officer Being Closely Guarded," *The Mobile Register* (Mobile, Alabama), April 2, 1921.

7. "Officers Raiding Mississippi Still Are Both Slain," *The Mobile Register* (Mobile, Alabama), April 2, 1921.

8. "Double Tragedy Marks Still Raid," *Greene County Herald* (Leakesville, Mississippi), April 8, 1921.

9. "Instanter Capias," John W. Colbert, Circuit Clerk, Greene County Circuit Court, Leakesville, Mississippi, May 9, 1921.

10. "Indictment: The State of Mississippi vs. Will Morris, Mancey F. Kelley, Henry A. Bond, John Adams, No. 969."

11. "Petition of Pardon," *Greene County Herald* (Leakesville, Mississippi), January 5, 1921.

12. "Mob Mutterings Sends Prisoners to Jackson Jail," *The Daily Herald* (Biloxi, Mississippi), April 6, 1921.

13. Ibid.

14. Ibid."

15. "Two Officers Killed While Raiding Still," *The Richton Dispatch* (Richton, Mississippi), April 8, 1921.

16. "Double Tragedy Marks Still Raid," *Greene County Herald.*

17. Ibid.

18. "Mob Mutterings Sends Prisoners to Jackson Jail."

CHAPTER THIRTEEN: SAVING HIS HIDE

1. "Circuit Court May Term 1921," *Greene County Herald* (Leakesville, Mississippi), May 27, 1921.

2. Working notes of Juanita Green Hollinghead.

3. Ibid.

4. "John Adams Given a Life Sentence," *The Richton Dispatch* (Richton, Mississippi), June 2, 1922.

5. *Legal Information Institute*, s.v. "continuance," Cornell Law School, accessed April 6, 2023, https://www.law.cornell.edu/wex/continuance.

6. "State of Mississippi vs. Johnie Adams, No. 967 & 968: Motion of Continuance," Greene County Circuit Court, Leakesville, Mississippi, May 27, 1922.

7. Ibid.

8. Ibid.

9. Ibid.

10. "John Adams Given a Life Sentence," *The Richton Dispatch.*

11. Ibid.

12. Ibid.

13. "Johnny Adams Trial," *Greene County Herald.*

14. "Johnnie Adams Trial Gets A Life Sentence," *Greene County Herald* (Leakesville, Mississippi), May 31, 1922.

15. Ibid.

16. Ibid.

17. "Handwritten jury instructions from John Adams' trial—No. 967," Greene County Circuit Court, Leakesville, Mississippi, May 27, 1922.

18. "Typewritten additional jury instructions from John Adams' trial—No. 967," Greene County Circuit Court, Leakesville, Mississippi, May 27, 1922.

19. "Johnny Adams Trial."

20. "Typewritten additional jury instructions from John Adams' trial—No. 967."

21. "Johnny Adams Trial."

22. "John Adams Given a Life Sentence."

23. Ibid.

CHAPTER FOURTEEN: NO FRIEND DEARER THAN JAKE

1. *Laws of the State of Mississippi Passed At A Special Session of The Mississippi Legislature* (Nashville: Press of Brandon Printing Company, 1910), p. 83.

2. Martin V. B. Miller to U.S. Senator Pat Harrison, December 12, 1919.

3. U.S. Senator Par Harrison to Jake Green, February 6, 1920.

4. Martin V. B. Miller to Eliza Green, December 23, 1921,

5. Ibid.

CHAPTER FIFTEEN: "GETHSEMANE"

1. "Modernization and Urban Renewal of Penn Street, Reading, PA," *Go Reading Berks*, accessed April 29, 2023, https://goreadingberks.com/modernization-and-urban-renewal-of-penn-street-reading-pa/.

2. "Self-Guided Walking Tour: Centre Park History District History," Center Park Historic District, accessed April 29, 2023, https://static1.squarespace.com/static/60c37ebbec338c7f30e2baf3/t/6181b1c603f65b7783d6e088/1635889607662/Walking+Tour+Map+and+Information.pdf.

3. Paul G. Kase to Mrs. Eliza Green, March 20, 1950.

4. "Apostles Creed," United Methodist Hymnal, United Methodist Church, accessed April 29, 2023, https://www.umc.org/en/content/apostles-creed-traditional-ecumenical.

CHAPTER TWENTY: WALKING IN THE SAME SHOES

1. "Illegal Wiskey Still Discovered in County: Second largest in Mississippi in last two decades," *Greene County Herald* (Leakesville, Mississippi), November 26, 1992.
2. Ibid.
3. Ibid.
4. "Jacob F. Green Is A Candidate For Sheriff Of County," *Greene County Herald* (Leakesville, Mississippi), January 17, 1947.

CHAPTER TWENTY-SIX: MY MISSISSIPPI MEN

1. Jim Harris, "A Notorious Killer Becomes a Folk Hero," *The Southern Voice*, accessed May 31, 2023, https://thesouthernvoice.com/a-notorious-killer-becomes-a-folk-hero-2/.
2. Ibid.

About the Authors

JUANITA GREEN HOLLINGHEAD
Author Juanita Green Hollinghead has devoted the last thirty-nine years of her life to uncovering the facts about the murder of her paternal grandfather. Since early childhood, Juanita has had an inexplicable yearning to know the whole story of Jake's death. Juanita's father never discussed the murder of his father with his wife or four children. Only in 1988, after her father's death, did Juanita begin an active personal investigation into this crime that shaped her entire family's history.

Juanita worked tirelessly for twenty-four years in the field of education in various positions—kindergarten, elementary, and junior high classroom instructor, instructional interventionist, principal, and independent consultant.

A fifth-generation Mississippian, Juanita has carried on the tradition of service to others established by other members of her Green family, including serving as a member of the Board of Alderman for the Town of Leakesville for eight years.

She and her husband, Andy, have two grown children—Drew and Paige—and three grandsons and five granddaughters. They attend Sonlight Community Church and make their home in Leakesville, Mississippi.

For more information, please visit
www.juanitagreenhollinghead.com

Follow her on Facebook at
Juanita Green Hollinghead

SHERYE S. GREEN

The writings of Sherye S. Green reflect her journey of faith and explore the heart's inner landscapes. An author, singer, and speaker, she has long been intrigued by the power of words to influence and shape thought and action. A former Miss Mississippi, Sherye has enjoyed two careers—one in business, the other in education. She is the award-winning author of two inspirational novels, *Abandon Not My Soul* and *Through a Dark Valley*, a devotional collection, *Tending the Garden of My Heart: Reflections on Cultivating a Life of Faith*, a World War II survivor memoir, *Surviving Hitler, Evading Stalin: One Woman's Remarkable Escape from Nazi Germany*, and *Mission Vigilant: A Mother's Crusade to Stem the Tide of Veteran Suicide*. Sherye is the 2021 Mississippi Author of the Year for Nonfiction.

Sherye and her husband make their home in Jackson, Mississippi. They are the parents of a son and daughter and are grandparents to five grandsons and one granddaughter.

For more information, please visit:
www.sheryesimmonsgreen.com

Follow her on Facebook at
Sherye Simmons Green

If Juanita's story has moved you and you would recommend it to others, please consider writing a review for *Beyond the Green Widow* on Amazon.com